AFGHANS on the double

W*hen you're ready to make an afghan but want to finish it fast, look to* Afghans on the Double. *You'll discover 52 cozy, captivating wraps — all worked holding two strands of yarn together for double-quick results.*

Packed with eye-pleasing creations, this indispensable collection features four terrific groupings. In Comfort on the Double, you'll find lots of casual throws touched with charm. Distinctively Double offers an array of classic and sophisticated styles. Sassy and fun describes the brightly colored throws in Double Play, and in Doubly Delightful there are sweet coverlets for sentimental settings.

Adapted from tried-and-true Leisure Arts patterns of all skill levels, this timeless treasury features afghans tailor-made for everyone you know — parents, grandparents, newlyweds, best friends, children, and especially you! Best of all, you can make them — on the double! — with our easy-to-follow instructions.

Twice as nice and double the fun, Afghans on the Double *is the answer for the busy crocheter!*

LEISURE ARTS, INC.
and
OXMOOR HOUSE, INC.

EDITORIAL STAFF

Vice President and Editor-in-Chief: Anne Van Wagner Childs
Executive Director: Sandra Graham Case
Executive Editor: Susan Frantz Wiles
Publications Director: Carla Bentley
Creative Art Director: Gloria Bearden
Production Art Director: Melinda Stout

PRODUCTION

Managing Editor: Susan White Sullivan
Technical Writer: Joan Gessner Beebe
Technical Editor: Linda Luder
Project Coordinator: Sarah J. Green

EDITORIAL

Associate Editor: Linda L. Trimble
Senior Editorial Writer: Robyn Sheffield-Edwards
Editorial Writer: Darla Burdette Kelsay
Editorial Associates: Tammi Williamson Bradley and Terri Leming Davidson
Copy Editor: Laura Lee Weland

ART

Book/Magazine Art Director: Diane M. Hugo
Senior Production Artist: M. Katherine Yancey
Production Art Assistant: Dana Vaughn
Photography Stylists: Christina Tiano Myers, Laura McCabe, Karen Smart Hall, Sondra Daniel, and Aurora Huston

BUSINESS STAFF

Publisher: Bruce Akin
Vice President, Finance: Tom Siebenmorgen
Vice President, Retail Sales: Thomas L. Carlisle
Retail Sales Director: Richard Tignor
Vice President, Retail Marketing: Pam Stebbins
Retail Customer Services Director: Margaret Sweetin
Marketing Manager: Russ Barnett
Executive Director of Marketing and Circulation: Guy A. Crossley
Circulation Manager: Byron L. Taylor
Print Production Manager: Laura Lockhart
Print Production Coordinator: Nancy Reddick Lister

Afghans on the Double
from the Crochet Treasury Series
Published by Leisure rts, Inc., and Oxmoor House, Inc.

Made in U.S.A.

Library of Congress Catalog Number 95-79984
Softcover ISBN 0-942237-90-0

Table Of Contents

Comfort On The Double...4

Distinctively Double.........38

Double Play..............68

Doubly Delightful..90

THE TAILOR OF
THE TALE OF

COMFORT ON THE DOUBLE

The warmth of a handmade afghan can whisk away all your cares and worries! Like tried and true friends, our casual wraps provide cozy companionship and pure comfort. No frills and no fuss make these selections extra easy to create and quick to finish. From ripples and grannies to cables and filet patterns, this carefree collection offers something to tickle everyone's fancy.

ZIGZAG FILET

An eye-pleasing filet pattern zigzags across this vibrant afghan. Crocheted in candy apple red yarn sprinkled with flecks of color, the wrap is finished with a simple tailored edging of single crochets.

Finished Size: Approximately 48" x 62"

MATERIALS

Worsted Weight Yarn, approximately:
40½ ounces, (1,150 grams, 2,660 yards)
Crochet hook, size P (10.00 mm) **or** size needed for gauge

Note: Each row is worked across length of Afghan holding two strands of yarn together.

GAUGE: 8 dc and 4 rows = 4"

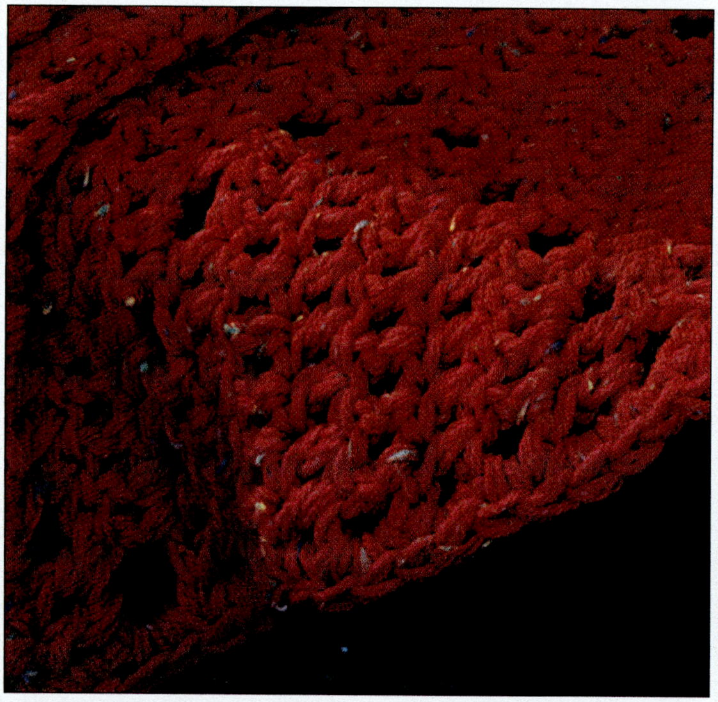

Ch 125 **loosely**.

Row 1 (Right side)**:** Dc in fourth ch from hook **(3 skipped chs count as first dc)** and in each ch across: 123 dc.

Row 2: Ch 4 **(counts as first dc plus ch 1, now and throughout)**, turn; skip next dc, dc in next 10 dc, ★ ch 1, skip next dc, dc in next 10 dc; repeat from ★ across to last 12 dc, ch 1, skip next dc, dc in last 11 dc: 11 ch-1 sps.

Row 3: Ch 3 **(counts as first dc, now and throughout)**, turn; ★ dc in next 8 dc, ch 1, skip next dc, dc in next dc and in next ch-1 sp; repeat from ★ across to last dc, dc in last dc.

Row 4: Ch 3, turn; dc in next 2 dc and in next ch-1 sp, dc in next dc, ★ ch 1, skip next dc, dc in next 8 dc, dc in next ch-1 sp and in next dc; repeat from ★ across to last 8 dc, ch 1, skip next dc, dc in last 7 dc.

Row 5: Ch 3, turn; dc in next 4 dc, ch 1, skip next dc, dc in next dc and in next ch-1 sp, ★ dc in next 8 dc, ch 1, skip next dc, dc in next dc and in next ch-1 sp; repeat from ★ across to last 5 dc, dc in last 5 dc.

Row 6: Ch 3, turn; dc in next 6 dc and in next ch-1 sp, dc in next dc, ★ ch 1, skip next dc, dc in next 8 dc, dc in next ch-1 sp and in next dc; repeat from ★ across to last 4 dc, ch 1, skip next dc, dc in last 3 dc.

Row 7: Ch 4, turn; skip next dc, dc in next dc and in next ch-1 sp, ★ dc in next 8 dc, ch 1, skip next dc, dc in next dc and in next ch-1 sp; repeat from ★ across to last 9 dc, dc in last 9 dc.

Rows 8-47: Repeat Rows 3-7, 8 times.

Row 48: Ch 3, turn; dc in next dc and in each dc and each ch-1 sp across; do **not** finish off.

EDGING

Ch 1, turn; sc evenly around working 3 sc in each corner; join with slip st to first sc, finish off.

CLASSIC CABLES

Featuring soft cables and ripples, this classic afghan is a welcome companion when snuggling down for a bedtime story.

Finished Size: Approximately 45" x 64"

MATERIALS

Worsted Weight Yarn, approximately:
61 ounces, (1,730 grams, 4,010 yards)
Crochet hook, size N (9.00 mm) **or** size needed for gauge

Note: Entire Afghan is worked holding two strands of yarn together.

GAUGE: In pattern, 9 dc and 5 rows = 4"
(9" point to point)

PATTERN STITCHES

BACK POST TREBLE CROCHET ***(abbreviated BPtr)***
YO twice, insert hook from **back** to **front** around post of st indicated, YO and pull up a loop (4 loops on hook) ***(Fig. 13, page 120)***, (YO and draw through 2 loops on hook) 3 times.

FRONT POST TREBLE CROCHET ***(abbreviated FPtr)***
YO twice, insert hook from **front** to **back** around post of st indicated, YO and pull up a loop (4 loops on hook) ***(Fig. 11, page 119)***, (YO and draw through 2 loops on hook) 3 times.

CABLE
Ch 5 **loosely**, slip st from **front** to **back** around post of dc indicated ***(Fig. 18a, page 121)***, turn; hdc in top loop of each ch just made ***(Fig. 18b, page 121)***. Do **not** skip dc behind Cable.

Ch 117 **loosely**.

Row 1 (Right side)**:** Dc in fifth ch from hook and in next 8 chs, 3 dc in next ch, ★ dc in next 10 chs, skip next 2 chs, dc in next 10 chs, 3 dc in next ch; repeat from ★ 3 times **more**, dc in next 9 chs, skip next ch, dc in last ch: 115 sts.

Note: Work in Back Loops Only throughout ***(Fig. 28, page 124)***.

Row 2: Ch 3 **(counts as first dc, now and throughout)**, turn; skip next dc, dc in next 9 dc, dc in next dc, work BPtr around same st, dc in same st, ★ dc in next 10 dc, skip next 2 dc, dc in next 10 dc, dc in next dc, work BPtr around same st, dc in same st; repeat from ★ 3 times **more**, dc in next 9 dc, skip next dc, dc in top of beginning ch: 115 sts.

Row 3: Ch 3, turn; skip next dc, dc in next 5 dc, work Cable around sixth st on Row 1, ★ † dc in next 4 dc, dc in next BPtr, work FPtr around same st, dc in same st, dc in next 5 dc, work Cable around fifth dc from last 3-dc group on Row 1 †, dc in next 5 dc, skip next 2 dc, dc in next 6 dc, work Cable around sixth dc from skipped chs on Row 1; repeat from ★ 3 times **more**, then repeat from † to † once, dc in next 4 dc, skip next dc, dc in last dc: 10 Cables.

Row 4: Ch 3, turn; skip next dc, dc in next 3 dc, ★ † skip next Cable, dc in next 6 dc, dc in next FPtr, work BPtr around same st, dc in same st, dc in next 5 dc †, skip next Cable, dc in next 5 dc, skip next 2 dc, dc in next 4 dc; repeat from ★ 3 times **more**, then repeat from † to † once, skip next Cable, dc in next 4 dc, skip next dc, dc in last dc: 115 sts.

Row 5: Ch 3, turn; skip next dc, dc in next 5 dc, work Cable around dc to **right** of Cable below ***(Fig. 19, page 121)***, ★ † dc in next 4 dc, dc in next BPtr, work FPtr around same st, dc in same st, dc in next 5 dc, work Cable around dc to **right** of Cable below †, dc in next 5 dc, skip next 2 dc, dc in next 6 dc, work Cable around dc to right of Cable below; repeat from ★ 3 times **more**, then repeat from † to † once, dc in next 4 dc, skip next dc, dc in last dc.

Repeat Rows 4 and 5 until Afghan measures approximately 64" from beginning ch, ending by working Row 4.
Finish off.

THE TAILOR OF GLOUCESTER
THE TALE OF PETER RABBIT

VINTAGE VIOLETS

Abloom with violet motifs, this quick-to-finish afghan presents an exquisite play on colors! The striking shades of purple stand out dramatically against the black borders of each square. This rich afghan is sure to be cherished and admired for many years.

Finished Size: Approximately 47½" x 66½"

MATERIALS

Worsted Weight Yarn, approximately:
Color A (Dark Purple) - 2½ ounces, (70 grams, 165 yards)
Color B (Purple) - 10 ounces, (280 grams, 655 yards)
Color C (Light Purple) - 21 ounces, (600 grams, 1,380 yards)
Color D (Black) - 29 ounces, (820 grams, 1,905 yards)
Crochet hook, size N (9.00 mm) **or** size needed for gauge
Yarn needle

Note: Entire Afghan is worked holding two strands of yarn together.

GAUGE: Each Square = 9½"

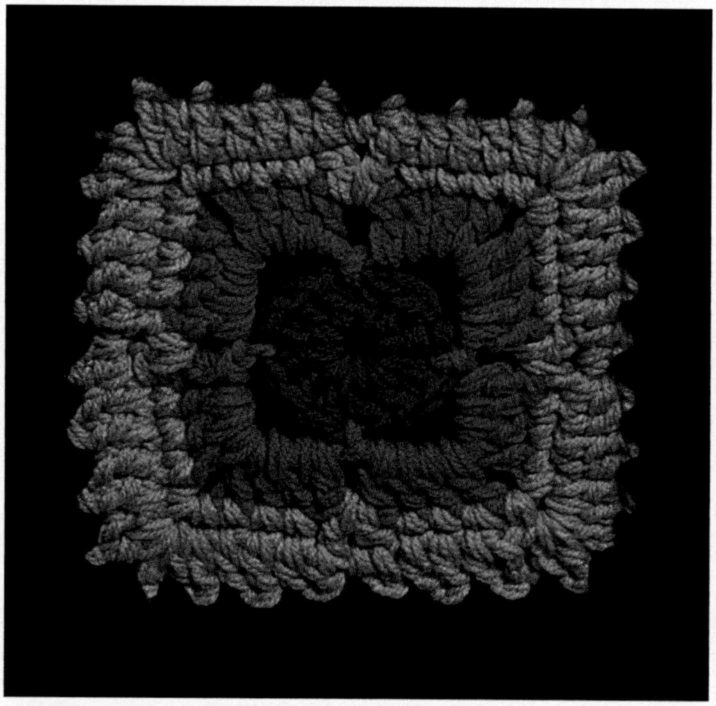

SQUARE (Make 35)

Rnd 1 (Right side)**:** With Color A, ch 4, 2 dc in fourth ch from hook, ch 1, (3 dc in same ch, ch 1) 3 times; join with slip st to top of beginning ch-4, finish off: 4 ch-1 sps.

Note: Loop a short piece of yarn around any stitch to mark last round as **right** side.

Rnd 2: With **right** side facing, join Color B with slip st in any ch-1 sp; ch 7, (slip st in next ch-1 sp, ch 7) around; join with slip st to first slip st: 4 loops.

Rnd 3: Slip st in first loop, ch 3 **(counts as first dc, now and throughout)**, (3 dc, ch 2, 4 dc) in same loop, ch 1, ★ (4 dc, ch 2, 4 dc) in next loop, ch 1; repeat from ★ around; join with slip st to first dc, finish off: 32 dc.

Rnd 4: With **right** side facing, join Color C with sc in any ch-2 sp ***(see Joining With Sc, page 124)***; ch 1, sc in same sp and in next 3 dc, skip next dc, (dc, ch 1, dc) in next ch-1 sp, skip next dc, sc in next 3 dc, ★ (sc, ch 1, sc) in next ch-2 sp, sc in next 3 dc, skip next dc, (dc, ch 1, dc) in next ch-1 sp, skip next dc, sc in next 3 dc; repeat from ★ around; join with slip st to first sc: 32 sc and 8 dc.

Rnd 5: Ch 3, (2 dc, ch 1, 2 dc) in next ch-1 sp, dc in next 5 sts, sc in next ch-1 sp, ★ dc in next 5 sts, (2 dc, ch 1, 2 dc) in next ch-1 sp, dc in next 5 sts, sc in next ch-1 sp; repeat from ★ around to last 4 sts, dc in last 4 sts; join with slip st to first dc, finish off: 56 dc.

Rnd 6: With **right** side facing, join Color D with slip st in any corner ch-1 sp; ch 3, (dc, ch 1, 2 dc) in same sp, skip next dc, (2 dc in next st, skip next dc) 7 times, ★ (2 dc, ch 1, 2 dc) in next ch-1 sp, skip next dc, (2 dc in next st, skip next dc) 7 times; repeat from ★ around; join with slip st to first dc: 72 dc.

Rnd 7: Slip st in next dc and in next ch-1 sp, ch 3, (dc, ch 1, 2 dc) in same sp, 2 sc in sp between each 2-dc group across to next corner ch-1 sp, ★ (2 dc, ch 1, 2 dc) in ch-1 sp, 2 sc in sp between each 2-dc group across to next corner ch-1 sp; repeat from ★ around; join with slip st to first dc, finish off: 64 sc.

ASSEMBLY

With Color D, whipstitch Squares together ***(Fig. 32a, page 125)*** forming 5 vertical strips of 7 Squares each, beginning in ch of first corner and ending in ch of next corner; then whipstitch strips together in same manner.

Photographs

OLD-FASHIONED CHARM

The perfect accompaniment for Early American decor, this engaging afghan is worked in blocks featuring raised stitches and Colonial colors. For easy assembly, the squares are whipstitched together in strips and completed with a simple edging.

Finished Size: Approximately 55" x 68"

MATERIALS

Worsted Weight Yarn, approximately:
MC (Blue) - 35½ ounces, (1,010 grams, 2,335 yards)
Color A (Red) - 8½ ounces, (240 grams, 560 yards)
Color B (Beige) - 6½ ounces, (180 grams, 425 yards)
Crochet hook, size P (10.00 mm) **or** size needed for gauge
Yarn needle

Note: Entire Afghan is worked holding two strands of yarn together.

GAUGE: Each Square = 13"

SQUARE (Make 20)

Rnd 1 (Right side)**:** With MC, ch 5, (dc, ch 1) 7 times in fifth ch from hook; join with slip st to fourth ch of beginning ch-5: 8 ch-1 sps.

Note: Loop a short piece of yarn around any stitch to mark last round as **right** side.

Rnd 2: Ch 3 **(counts as first dc, now and throughout)**, (dc, ch 3, dc) in next ch-1 sp, dc in next dc, ch 1, ★ dc in next dc, (dc, ch 3, dc) in next ch-1 sp, dc in next dc, ch 1; repeat from ★ around; join with slip st to first dc, finish off: 4 ch-3 sps.

Rnd 3: With **right** side facing, join Color A with sc in any ch-3 sp ***(see Joining With Sc, page 124)***; ch 3, sc in same sp and in next 2 dc, ch 3, sc in next 2 dc, ★ (sc, ch 3, sc) in next ch-3 sp (corner), sc in next 2 dc, ch 3, sc in next 2 dc; repeat from ★ around; join with slip st to first sc, finish off: 8 ch-3 sps.

Rnd 4: With **right** side facing, join Color B with sc in any corner ch-3 sp; ch 2, sc in same sp and in next 3 sc, working **behind** next ch-3, dc in ch-1 sp on Rnd 2, sc in next 3 sc, ★ (sc, ch 2, sc) in next corner ch-3 sp, sc in next 3 sc, working **behind** next ch-3, dc in ch-1 sp on Rnd 2, sc in next 3 sc; repeat from ★ around; join with slip st to first sc, finish off: 36 sts and 4 ch-2 sps.

Rnd 5: With **right** side facing, join MC with slip st in any corner ch-2 sp; ch 5 **(counts as first dc plus ch 2)**, dc in same sp and in next sc, (ch 1, skip next sc, dc in next st) 4 times, ★ (dc, ch 2, dc) in next corner ch-2 sp, dc in next sc, (ch 1, skip next sc, dc in next st) 4 times; repeat from ★ around; join with slip st to first dc, finish off: 28 dc.

Rnd 6: With **right** side facing, join Color A with sc in any corner ch-2 sp; ch 2, sc in same sp and in next 2 dc, sc in next ch-1 sp and in next dc, 3 tr in next ch-3 sp on Rnd 3, skip next dc (behind 3-tr group), sc in next dc, sc in next ch-1 sp and in next 2 dc, ★ (sc, ch 2, sc) in next corner ch-2 sp, sc in next 2 dc, sc in next ch-1 sp and in next dc, 3 tr in next ch-3 sp on Rnd 3, skip next dc (behind 3-tr group), sc in next dc, sc in next ch-1 sp and in next 2 dc; repeat from ★ around; join with slip st to first sc, finish off: 52 sts and 4 ch-2 sps.

Rnd 7: With **right** side facing, join Color B with sc in any corner ch-2 sp; ch 2, sc in same sp and in next 5 sc, ch 3, skip next 3 tr, sc in next 5 sc, ★ (sc, ch 2, sc) in next corner ch-2 sp, sc in next 5 sc, ch 3, skip next 3 tr, sc in next 5 sc; repeat from ★ around; join with slip st to first sc, finish off: 48 sc.

Rnd 8: With **right** side facing, join MC with slip st in any corner ch-2 sp; ch 6 **(counts as first dc plus ch 3)**, dc in same sp and in next 6 sc, 3 dc in next ch-3 sp, dc in next 6 sc, ★ (dc, ch 3, dc) in next corner ch-2 sp, dc in next 6 sc, 3 dc in next ch-3 sp, dc in next 6 sc; repeat from ★ around; join with slip st to first dc: 68 dc.

Rnd 9: Ch 3, (dc, ch 3, dc) in corner ch-3 sp, ★ dc in next dc and in each dc across to next corner ch-3 sp, (dc, ch 3, dc) in corner ch-3 sp; repeat from ★ 2 times **more**, dc in each dc across; join with slip st to first dc, finish off.

ASSEMBLY

With MC, whipstitch Squares together ***(Fig. 32a, page 125)*** forming 4 vertical strips of 5 Squares each, beginning in center ch of first corner and ending in center ch of next corner; then whipstitch strips together in same manner.

EDGING

Rnd 1: With **right** side facing, join MC with sc in any corner ch-3 sp; 2 sc in same sp, working in Back Loops Only ***(Fig. 28, page 124)***, sc in each dc, in each sp, and in each joining around working 3 sc in each corner ch-3 sp; join with slip st to **both** loops of first sc.

Rnd 2: Ch 3, working in both loops, 3 dc in next sc, ★ dc in each sc across to center sc of next corner, 3 dc in corner sc; repeat from ★ 2 times **more**, dc in each sc across; join with slip st to first dc, finish off.

DOUBLE STAIR STEP

Stitched in yarn as blue as a clear autumn sky, this cozy throw will brighten any quiet corner. Diagonal rows of openwork create the stair-step pattern.

Finished Size: Approximately 50" x 66"

MATERIALS

Worsted Weight Yarn, approximately:
50 ounces, (1,360 grams, 3,155 yards)
Crochet hook, size N (9.00 mm) **or** size needed for gauge

Note: Each row is worked across length of Afghan holding two strands of yarn together.

GAUGE: 9 dc and 5 rows = 4"

Ch 146 **loosely**.

Row 1 (Right side)**:** Dc in fourth ch from hook **(3 skipped chs count as first dc)** and in next 6 chs, ch 2, skip next 2 chs, dc in next 4 chs, ★ ch 2, skip next 2 chs, dc in next 10 chs, ch 2, skip next 2 chs, dc in next 4 chs; repeat from ★ across to last 4 chs, ch 2, skip next 2 chs, dc in last 2 chs: 16 ch-2 sps.

Note: Loop a short piece of yarn around any stitch to mark last row as **right** side.

Row 2: Ch 3 **(counts as first dc, now and throughout)**, turn; dc in next dc, 2 dc in next sp, ch 2, skip next 2 dc, dc in next 2 dc, 2 dc in next sp, ★ ch 2, skip next 2 dc, dc in next 8 dc, 2 dc in next sp, ch 2, skip next 2 dc, dc in next 2 dc, 2 dc in next sp; repeat from ★ across to last 8 dc, ch 2, skip next 2 dc, dc in last 6 dc.

Row 3: Ch 3, turn; dc in next 3 dc, ch 2, 2 dc in next sp, dc in next 2 dc, ch 2, 2 dc in next sp, ★ dc in next 8 dc, ch 2, 2 dc in next sp, dc in next 2 dc, ch 2, 2 dc in next sp; repeat from ★ across to last 4 dc, dc in last 4 dc.

Row 4: Ch 3, turn; dc in next 5 dc, 2 dc in next sp, ch 2, skip next 2 dc, dc in next 2 dc, 2 dc in next sp, ★ ch 2, skip next 2 dc, dc in next 8 dc, 2 dc in next sp, ch 2, skip next 2 dc, dc in next 2 dc, 2 dc in next sp; repeat from ★ across to last 4 dc, ch 2, skip next 2 dc, dc in last 2 dc.

Row 5: Ch 3, turn; dc in next dc, 2 dc in next sp, dc in next 2 dc, ch 2, 2 dc in next sp, dc in next 8 dc, ★ ch 2, 2 dc in next sp, dc in next 2 dc, ch 2, 2 dc in next sp, dc in next 8 dc; repeat from ★ across.

Row 6: Ch 3, turn; dc in next 9 dc, 2 dc in next sp, ★ ch 2, skip next 2 dc, dc in next 2 dc, 2 dc in next sp, ch 2, skip next 2 dc, dc in next 8 dc, 2 dc in next sp; repeat from ★ across to last 6 dc, ch 2, skip next 2 dc, dc in last 4 dc.

Row 7: Ch 3, turn; dc in next dc, ch 2, 2 dc in next sp, dc in next 8 dc, ★ ch 2, 2 dc in next sp, dc in next 2 dc, ch 2, 2 dc in next sp, dc in next 8 dc; repeat from ★ across to last 4 dc, ch 2, skip next 2 dc, dc in last 2 dc.

Row 8: Ch 3, turn; dc in next dc, 2 dc in next sp, ch 2, skip next 2 dc, dc in next 8 dc, 2 dc in next sp, ★ ch 2, skip next 2 dc, dc in next 2 dc, 2 dc in next sp, ch 2, skip next 2 dc, dc in next 8 dc, 2 dc in next sp; repeat from ★ across to last 2 dc, dc in last 2 dc.

Row 9: Ch 3, turn; dc in next 9 dc, ch 2, 2 dc in next sp, ★ dc in next 2 dc, ch 2, 2 dc in next sp, dc in next 8 dc, ch 2, 2 dc in next sp; repeat from ★ across to last 4 dc, dc in last 4 dc.

Row 10: Ch 3, turn; dc in next dc, ch 2, skip next 2 dc, dc in next 2 dc, 2 dc in next sp, ★ ch 2, skip next 2 dc, dc in next 8 dc, 2 dc in next sp, ch 2, skip next 2 dc, dc in next 2 dc, 2 dc in next sp; repeat from ★ across to last 10 dc, ch 2, skip next 2 dc, dc in last 8 dc.

Row 11: Ch 3, turn; dc in next 5 dc, ch 2, 2 dc in next sp, dc in next 2 dc, ch 2, 2 dc in next sp, ★ dc in next 8 dc, ch 2, 2 dc in next sp, dc in next 2 dc, ch 2, 2 dc in next sp; repeat from ★ across to last 2 dc, dc in last 2 dc.

Row 12: Ch 3, turn; dc in next 3 dc, 2 dc in next sp, ch 2, skip next 2 dc, dc in next 2 dc, 2 dc in next sp, ★ ch 2, skip next 2 dc, dc in next 8 dc, 2 dc in next sp, ch 2, skip next 2 dc, dc in next 2 dc, 2 dc in next sp; repeat from ★ across to last 6 dc, ch 2, skip next 2 dc, dc in last 4 dc.

Row 13: Ch 3, turn; dc in next dc, ch 2, 2 dc in next sp, dc in next 2 dc, ch 2, 2 dc in next sp, ★ dc in next 8 dc, ch 2, 2 dc in next sp, dc in next 2 dc, ch 2, 2 dc in next sp; repeat from ★ across to last 6 dc, dc in last 6 dc.

Row 14: Ch 3, turn; dc in next 7 dc, 2 dc in next sp, ch 2, skip next 2 dc, dc in next 2 dc, 2 dc in next sp, ★ ch 2, skip next 2 dc, dc in next 8 dc, 2 dc in next sp, ch 2, skip next 2 dc, dc in next 2 dc, 2 dc in next sp; repeat from ★ across to last 2 dc, dc in last 2 dc.

Row 15: Ch 3, turn; dc in next 3 dc, ch 2, 2 dc in next sp, ★ dc in next 8 dc, ch 2, 2 dc in next sp, dc in next 2 dc, ch 2, 2 dc in next sp; repeat from ★ across to last 10 dc, dc in last 10 dc.

Row 16: Ch 3, turn; dc in next dc, ch 2, skip next 2 dc, dc in next 8 dc, 2 dc in next sp, ★ ch 2, skip next 2 dc, dc in next 2 dc, 2 dc in next sp, ch 2, skip next 2 dc, dc in next 8 dc, 2 dc in next sp; repeat from ★ across to last 4 dc, ch 2, skip next 2 dc, dc in last 2 dc.

Row 17: Ch 3, turn; dc in next dc, 2 dc in next sp, dc in next 8 dc, ch 2, 2 dc in next sp, dc in next 2 dc, ★ ch 2, 2 dc in next sp, dc in next 8 dc, ch 2, 2 dc in next sp, dc in next 2 dc; repeat from ★ across.
Row 18: Ch 3, turn; dc in next 3 dc, 2 dc in next sp, ★ ch 2, skip next 2 dc, dc in next 8 dc, 2 dc in next sp, ch 2, skip next 2 dc, dc in next 2 dc, 2 dc in next sp; repeat from ★ across to last 12 dc, ch 2, skip next 2 dc, dc in last 10 dc.
Row 19: Ch 3, turn; dc in next 7 dc, ch 2, 2 dc in next sp, dc in next 2 dc, ★ ch 2, 2 dc in next sp, dc in next 8 dc, ch 2, 2 dc in next sp, dc in next 2 dc; repeat from ★ across to last 4 dc, ch 2, skip next 2 dc, dc in last 2 dc.

Repeat Rows 2-19 until Afghan measures approximately 48" from beginning ch, ending by working a **wrong** side row; do **not** finish off.

EDGING

Rnd 1: Ch 1, turn; sc evenly around working 5 sc in each corner; join with slip st to first sc.
Rnd 2: Ch 3, do **not** turn; dc in next sc and in each sc around; join with slip st to first dc; finish off.

HEARTHSIDE DIAMONDS

This hearthside wrap will provide lots of warmth during cold winter nights! Popcorn diamonds and ridges of reverse crochet add generous texture to the tranquil teal afghan. For a polished finish, it's edged with reverse single crochets.

Finished Size: Approximately 56" x 65"

MATERIALS

Worsted Weight Yarn, approximately:
88 ounces, (2,500 grams, 6,035 yards)
Crochet hook, size N (9.00 mm) **or** size needed for gauge

Note: Each row is worked across length of Afghan holding two strands of yarn together.

GAUGE: 9 dc and 5 rows = 4"

Ch 149 **loosely**.
Row 1 (Right side)**:** Dc in fourth ch from hook **(3 skipped chs count as first dc)** and in each ch across: 147 dc.
Note: Loop a short piece of yarn around any stitch to mark last row as **right** side.
Row 2: Ch 1, do **not** turn; working from **left** to **right** and in Front Loops Only ***(Fig. 28, page 124)***, work reverse sc in each dc across ***(Figs. 26a-d, page 123)***.
Row 3: Ch 3 **(counts as first dc, now and throughout)**, do **not** turn; working in free loops of previous row ***(Fig. 29, page 124)***, dc in next st and in each st across.
Rows 4-9: Repeat Rows 2 and 3, 3 times.
Row 10: Ch 3, turn; dc in next dc and in each dc across.
Note: To work **Popcorn**, 5 dc in next dc, drop loop from hook, insert hook in first dc of 5-dc group, hook dropped loop and draw through ***(Fig. 8b, page 119)***, ch 1 to close.
Row 11: Ch 3, turn; dc in next 6 dc, work Popcorn, ★ dc in next 11 dc, work Popcorn; repeat from ★ across to last 7 dc, dc in last 7 dc: 12 Popcorns.
Row 12: Ch 3, turn; dc in next dc and in each st across: 147 dc.
Row 13: Ch 3, turn; dc in next 4 dc, work Popcorn, dc in next 3 dc, work Popcorn, ★ dc in next 7 dc, work Popcorn, dc in next 3 dc, work Popcorn; repeat from ★ across to last 5 dc, dc in last 5 dc: 24 Popcorns.
Row 14: Ch 3, turn; dc in next dc and in each st across: 147 dc.
Row 15: Ch 3, turn; dc in next 2 dc, ★ work Popcorn, dc in next 3 dc; repeat from ★ across: 36 Popcorns.
Row 16: Ch 3, turn; dc in next dc and in each st across: 147 dc.
Rows 17 and 18: Repeat Rows 13 and 14.
Row 19: Repeat Row 11.
Rows 20 and 21: Ch 3, turn; dc in next dc and in each st across.
Repeat Rows 2-21 until Afghan measures approximately $54^1/2$", ending by working Row 9; do **not** finish off.

EDGING

Rnd 1: Ch 1, do **not** turn; sc evenly around working 3 sc in each corner; join with slip st to first sc.
Rnd 2: Ch 1, do **not** turn; working from **left** to **right**, work reverse sc in both loops of each sc around; join with slip st to first st, finish off.

RUGGED WRAP

Worked entirely in the simplest crochet stitches, this handsome throw is easy to make and quick to finish. The afghan's rugged appeal makes it ideal for a cabin hideaway or a country lodge. Long fringe accents the ends.

Finished Size: Approximately 46" x 60"

MATERIALS

Worsted Weight Yarn, approximately:
MC (Brown) - 41 ounces, (1,160 grams, 2,575 yards)
Colors A thru D (Rust, Ecru, Green, and Tan)
7 ounces, (200 grams, 440 yards) **each**
Crochet hook, size P (10.00 mm) **or** size needed for gauge

Note: Each row is worked across length of Afghan holding two strands of yarn together. When joining yarn and finishing off, leave an 8" length at end to be worked into fringe.

GAUGE: In pattern, 16 sts = 7" and 8 rows = 4"

STRIPE SEQUENCE

2 Rows MC, ★ 1 row **each** of Color A, MC, Color B, MC, Color C, MC, Color D, MC; repeat from ★ throughout.

With MC, ch 137 **loosely**.

Row 1 (Right side)**:** Sc in second ch from hook and in each ch across; finish off: 136 sc.

Note: Loop a short piece of yarn around any stitch to mark last row as **right** side.

Row 2: With **wrong** side facing, join MC with sc in first sc ***(see Joining With Sc, page 124)***; ★ ch 2, skip next 2 sc, sc in next 2 sc; repeat from ★ across to last 3 sc, ch 2, skip next 2 sc, sc in last sc; finish off: 68 sc and 34 ch-2 sps.

Row 3: With **right** side facing, join yarn with sc in first sc; working in **front** of next ch-2, dc in next 2 sts one row **below**, ★ ch 2, skip next 2 sts, working in **front** of next ch-2, dc in next 2 sts one row **below**; repeat from ★ across to last sc, sc in last sc; finish off: 136 sts.

Row 4: With **wrong** side facing, join MC with sc in first sc; ★ ch 2, skip next 2 dc, working **behind** next ch-2, dc in next 2 sts one row **below**; repeat from ★ across to last 3 sts, ch 2, skip next 2 dc, sc in last sc; finish off.

Repeat Rows 3 and 4 until Afghan measures approximately 45" from beginning ch, ending by working Row 3 with Color D.

Last Row: With **wrong** side facing, join MC with sc in first sc; ★ sc in next 2 dc, working **behind** next ch-2, dc in next 2 sts one row **below**; repeat from ★ across to last 3 sts, sc in last 3 sts; do **not** finish off.

Edging - First Side: Ch 1, turn; slip st in first sc, ★ ch 2, dc in next st, skip next st, slip st in next st; repeat from ★ across; finish off.

Edging - Second Side: With **right** side facing and working in free loops of beginning ch ***(Fig. 29b, page 124)***, join MC with slip st in first ch; ★ ch 2, dc in next ch, skip next ch, slip st in next ch; repeat from ★ across; finish off.

Add additional fringe to each end ***(Figs. 33b & d, page 126)***, using two 18" strands of corresponding color.

RUSTIC RAISED CHEVRON

Fashioned with double crochets, this traditional chevron throw has a rich, rustic feel. Textured ripples, worked with variegated yarn in muted colors, are stitched between rows of deep forest green.

Finished Size: Approximately 50" x 68"

MATERIALS

Worsted Weight Yarn, approximately:
MC (Dark Green) - 41 ounces,
(1,160 grams, 3,045 yards)
CC (Variegated) - 11 ounces, (310 grams, 815 yards)
Crochet hook, size N (9.00 mm) **or** size needed for gauge

Note: Entire Afghan is worked holding two strands of yarn together.

GAUGE: One repeat (point to point) = $4^1/_2$"
and 4 rows = 4"

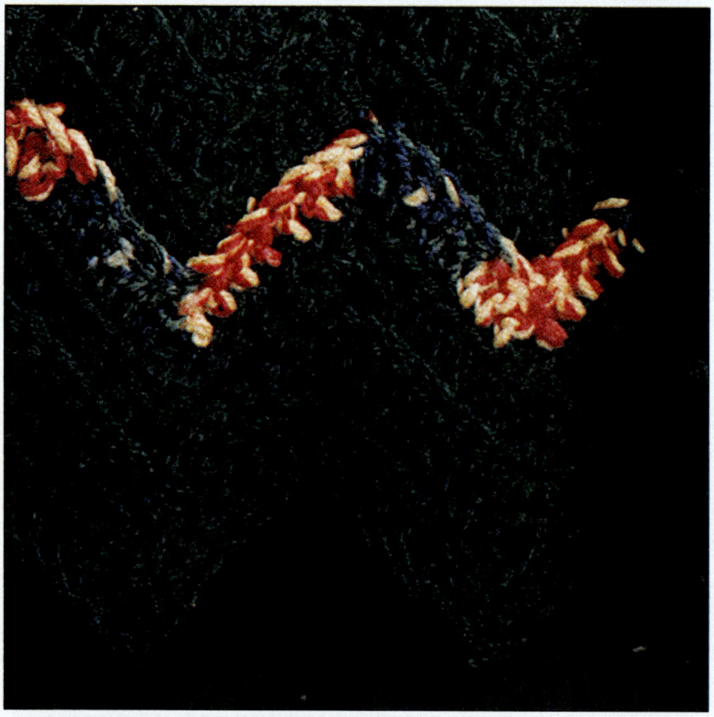

PATTERN STITCHES

CLUSTER (uses next 5 sts)
YO, insert hook in next st, YO and pull up a loop, YO and draw through 2 loops on hook, YO, skip next 3 sts, insert hook in next st, YO and pull up a loop, YO and draw through 2 loops on hook, YO and draw through all 3 loops on hook ***(Figs. 16c & d, page 120)***.

DC DECREASE (uses next 3 sts)
YO, insert hook in next st, YO and pull up a loop, YO and draw through 2 loops on hook, skip next st, YO, insert hook in next st, YO and pull up a loop, YO and draw through 2 loops on hook, YO and draw through all 3 loops on hook ***(Fig. 23, page 122)***.

SHELL
(2 Dc, ch 1, 2 dc) in next st or ch-1 sp.

STRIPE SEQUENCE

3 Rows MC ***(Fig. 30a, page 124)***, ★ 1 row CC, 3 rows MC; repeat from ★ throughout.

With MC, ch 179 **loosely**.
Row 1 (Right side)**:** YO, insert hook in fourth ch from hook (**3 skipped chs count as first dc**), YO and pull up a loop, YO and draw through 2 loops on hook, YO, insert hook in next ch, YO and pull up a loop, YO and draw through 2 loops on hook, YO and draw through all 3 loops on hook, dc in next 5 chs, work Shell, dc in next 5 chs, ★ work Cluster, dc in next 5 chs, work Shell, dc in next 5 chs; repeat from ★ across to last 3 chs, (YO, insert hook in **next** ch, YO and pull up a loop, YO and draw through 2 loops on hook) twice, YO and draw through all 3 loops on hook, dc in last ch: 168 sts.
Note: Loop a short piece of yarn around any stitch to mark last row as **right** side.
Row 2: Ch 3 **(counts as first dc, now and throughout)**, turn; working in Front Loops Only ***(Fig. 28, page 124)***, dc decrease, dc in next 5 dc, work Shell, dc in next 5 dc, ★ work Cluster, dc in next 5 dc, work Shell, dc in next 5 dc; repeat from ★ across to last 4 dc, dc decrease, dc in last dc.
Row 3: Ch 3, turn; working in Back Loops Only, dc decrease, dc in next 5 dc, work Shell, dc in next 5 dc, ★ work Cluster, dc in next 5 dc, work Shell, dc in next 5 dc; repeat from ★ across to last 4 dc, dc decrease, dc in last dc.
Repeat Rows 2 and 3 until Afghan measures approximately 68" from beginning ch, ending by working 3 rows MC.
Finish off.

A STUDY IN COMFORT

Double crochet and long double crochet stitches create a leaflike pattern on this comfy afghan for him. Made with brushed acrylic yarn, it's incredibly soft. Simple chain loops edge the handsome wrap.

Finished Size: Approximately 46 1/2" x 60"

MATERIALS

Worsted Weight Brushed Acrylic Yarn, approximately:
MC (Green) - 19 ounces, (540 grams, 1,465 yards)
CC (Tan) - 18 ounces, (510 grams, 1,390 yards)
Crochet hook, size P (10.00 mm) **or** size needed for gauge

Note: Entire Afghan is worked holding two strands of yarn together.

GAUGE: In pattern, 8 dc = 4" and 4 rows = 3 1/2"

With CC, ch 85 **loosely**.
Row 1 (Right side)**:** Dc in fourth ch from hook **(3 skipped chs count as first dc)** and in next ch, ★ ch 1, skip next ch, dc in next 3 chs; repeat from ★ across: 20 ch-1 sps.
Note: Loop a short piece of yarn around any stitch to mark last row as **right** side.
Row 2: Ch 3 **(counts as first dc, now and throughout)**, turn; dc in next 2 dc, ★ ch 1, dc in next 3 dc; repeat from ★ across changing to MC in last dc *(**Fig. 30a, page 124**)*.

Note: To work **Long double crochet *(abbreviated Ldc)***, YO, insert hook in ch-1 sp one row **below** next ch-1 sp *(**Fig. 14b, page 120**)*, YO and pull up a loop even with last st made, (YO and draw through 2 loops on hook) twice.
Row 3: Ch 4 **(counts as first dc plus ch 1, now and throughout)**, turn; skip next dc, dc in next dc, ★ work Ldc, dc in next dc, ch 1, skip next dc, dc in next dc; repeat from ★ across: 21 ch-1 sps.
Row 4: Ch 4, turn; skip next ch-1 sp, dc in next 3 sts, ★ ch 1, skip next ch-1 sp, dc in next 3 sts; repeat from ★ across to last ch-1 sp, ch 1, skip last ch-1 sp, dc in last dc changing to CC.
Row 5: Ch 3, turn; work Ldc, dc in next dc, ★ ch 1, skip next dc, dc in next dc, work Ldc, dc in next dc; repeat from ★ across: 20 ch-1 sps.
Row 6: Ch 3, turn; dc in next 2 sts, ★ ch 1, skip next ch-1 sp, dc in next 3 sts; repeat from ★ across changing to MC in last dc.
Repeat Rows 3-6 until Afghan measures approximately 55" from beginning ch, ending by working Row 6.

EDGING

Rnd 1: Ch 1, turn; 3 sc in first dc, sc in each dc and in each ch-1 sp across to last 2 dc, skip next dc, 3 sc in last dc; work 110 sc evenly spaced across end of rows; working in free loops of beginning ch *(**Fig. 29b, page 124**)*, 3 sc in first ch, sc in next 80 chs, skip next ch, 3 sc in next ch; work 110 sc evenly spaced across end of rows; join with slip st to first sc: 392 sc.
Rnd 2: Ch 3, do **not** turn; 3 dc in next sc, dc in each sc around working 3 dc in each corner sc; join with slip st to first dc, finish off: 400 dc.
Rnd 3: With **right** side facing, join CC with slip st in any dc; ch 1, sc in each dc around working 3 sc in each corner dc; join with slip st to first sc, finish off: 408 sc.
Rnd 4: With **right** side facing, join MC with slip st in any corner sc; ch 1, (sc in same st, ch 5) twice, skip next 2 sc, (sc in next sc, ch 5, skip next 2 sc) across to next corner sc, ★ (sc, ch 5) twice in corner sc, skip next 2 sc, (sc in next sc, ch 5, skip next 2 sc) across to next corner sc; repeat from ★ around; join with slip st to first sc, finish off.

GRANNY'S DELIGHT

Super-quick granny squares are joined into strips to make this pretty afghan. Finished with a graceful scalloped edging, the throw is a delightful variation of the traditional pattern.

Finished Size: Approximately 48½" x 60½"

MATERIALS

Worsted Weight Yarn, approximately:
- MC (Black) - 46 ounces, (1,310 grams, 2,225 yards)
- Color A (Dark Pink) - 3 ounces, (90 grams, 145 yards)
- Color B (Pink) - 4 ounces, (110 grams, 195 yards)
- Color C (Dark Blue) - 3 ounces, (90 grams, 145 yards)
- Color D (Blue) - 4 ounces, (110 grams, 195 yards)
- Color E (Dark Green) - 1½ ounces, (40 grams, 70 yards)
- Color F (Green) - 2 ounces, (60 grams, 95 yards)

Crochet hook, size N (9.00 mm) **or** size needed for gauge
Yarn needle

Note: Entire Afghan is worked holding two strands of yarn together.

GAUGE: Each Square = 4"
Each Strip = 9" x 57"

STRIP A

SQUARE A (Make 26)

Rnd 1 (Right side)**:** With Color A, ch 4, 2 dc in fourth ch from hook, ch 3, (3 dc in same ch, ch 3) 3 times; join with slip st to top of beginning ch-4, finish off: 4 ch-3 sps.

Note: Loop a short piece of yarn around any stitch to mark last round as **right** side.

Rnd 2: With **right** side facing, join MC with slip st in any ch-3 sp; ch 3 **(counts as first dc, now and throughout)**, (2 dc, ch 3, 3 dc) in same sp, ch 1, ★ (3 dc, ch 3, 3 dc) in next ch-3 sp, ch 1; repeat from ★ around; join with slip st to first dc, finish off.

JOINING

With MC, whipstitch Squares together ***(Fig. 32b, page 125)*** forming 2 vertical Strips of 13 Squares each, beginning in center ch of first corner and ending in center ch of next corner; do **not** join Strips.

EDGING

Rnd 1: With **right** side facing, join MC with sc in top **right** ch-3 sp ***(see Joining With Sc, page 124)***; ch 3, sc in same sp, ch 1, † skip next dc, sc in next dc, ch 1, sc in next ch-1 sp, ch 1, skip next dc, sc in next dc, ch 1, (sc, ch 3, sc) in next ch-3 sp, ch 1, skip next dc, sc in next dc, ch 1, sc in next ch-1 sp, ch 1, skip next dc, sc in next dc, ch 1, [(sc in next sp, ch 1) twice, skip next dc, sc in next dc, ch 1, sc in next ch-1 sp, ch 1, skip next dc, sc in next dc, ch 1] across to next ch-3 sp †, (sc, ch 3, sc) in ch-3 sp, ch 1, repeat from † to † once; join with slip st to first sc: 140 sps.

Rnd 2: Slip st in first ch-3 sp, ch 1, (sc, ch 3, sc) in same sp, ch 1, (sc in next ch-1 sp, ch 1) across to next ch-3 sp, ★ (sc, ch 3, sc) in ch-3 sp, ch 1, (sc in next ch-1 sp, ch 1) across to next ch-3 sp; repeat from ★ around; join with slip st to first sc, finish off: 144 sps.

Rnd 3: With **right** side facing, join Color B with slip st in top **right** ch-3 sp; ch 3, (2 dc, ch 3, 3 dc) in same sp, ch 1, skip next ch-1 sp, (3 dc in next ch-1 sp, ch 1, skip next ch-1 sp) across to next ch-3 sp, ★ (3 dc, ch 3, 3 dc) in ch-3 sp, ch 1, skip next ch-1 sp, (3 dc in next ch-1 sp, ch 1, skip next ch-1 sp) across to next ch-3 sp; repeat from ★ around; join with slip st to first dc, finish off.

Rnd 4: With **right** side facing, join MC with slip st in any ch-3 sp; ch 3, (2 dc, ch 3, 3 dc) in same sp, ch 1, (3 dc in next ch-1 sp, ch 1) across to next ch-3 sp, ★ (3 dc, ch 3, 3 dc) in ch-3 sp, ch 1, (3 dc in next ch-1 sp, ch 1) across to next ch-3 sp; repeat from ★ around; join with slip st to first dc, finish off.

STRIP B

SQUARE B (Make 26)

Work same as Square A working in the following color sequence: One rnd **each** of Color C and MC.

JOINING

Work same as Strip A.

EDGING

Work same as Strip A working in the following color sequence: 2 Rnds MC, 1 rnd **each** of Color D and MC.

STRIP C

SQUARE C (Make 13)

Work same as Square A working in the following color sequence: One rnd **each** of Color E and MC.

JOINING

Work in same manner as Strip A, forming one vertical strip.

EDGING

Work same as Strip A working in the following color sequence: 2 Rnds MC, 1 rnd **each** of Color F and MC.

ASSEMBLY

Whipstitch Strips together in the following order: A-B-C-B-A.

BORDER

Rnd 1: With **right** side facing, join MC with sc in top **right** ch-3 sp; ch 3, sc in same sp, ch 1, † skip next dc, sc in next dc, ch 1, (sc in next ch-1 sp, ch 1, skip next dc, sc in next dc, ch 1) 4 times, ★ (sc in next sp, ch 1) twice, skip next dc, sc in next dc, ch 1, (sc in next ch-1 sp, ch 1, skip next dc, sc in next dc, ch 1) 4 times; repeat from ★ across to next ch-3 sp, (sc, ch 3, sc) in ch-3 sp, ch 1, skip next dc, sc in next dc, ch 1, (sc in next ch-1 sp, ch 1, skip next dc, sc in next dc, ch 1) across to next ch-3 sp †, (sc, ch 3, sc) in ch-3 sp, ch 1, repeat from † to † once; join with slip st to first sc.

Rnd 2: Slip st in first ch-3 sp, ch 1, (sc, ch 3, sc) in same sp, ch 1, (sc in next ch-1 sp, ch 1) across to next ch-3 sp, ★ (sc, ch 3, sc) in ch-3 sp, ch 1, (sc in next ch-1 sp, ch 1) across to next ch-3 sp; repeat from ★ around; join with slip st to first sc.

Note #1: To work **Lace St**, ch 3, dc in third ch from hook.

Note #2: To work **Corner Lace St**, sc in sp indicated, ch 4, dc in fourth ch from hook, sc in same sp.

Rnd 3: Slip st in first ch-3 sp, ch 1, work Corner Lace St in same sp, work Lace St, skip next ch-1 sp, (sc in next ch-1 sp, work Lace St, skip next ch-1 sp) across to next ch-3 sp, ★ work Corner Lace St in ch-3 sp, work Lace St, skip next ch-1 sp, (sc in next ch-1 sp, work Lace St, skip next ch-1 sp) across to next ch-3 sp; repeat from ★ around; join with slip st to first sc, finish off.

LACY PINEAPPLES

Worked in panels featuring lacy pineapples, an Early American symbol of hospitality, this quick-to-finish throw has welcoming appeal wherever it's displayed.

Finished Size: Approximately 47"x 68"

MATERIALS

Worsted Weight Yarn, approximately:
53 ounces, (1,510 grams, 3,485 yards)
Crochet hook, size P (10.00 mm) **or** size needed for gauge
Yarn needle

Note: Entire Afghan is worked holding two strands of yarn together.

GAUGE: 9 dc and 5 rows = 4"

Note: To work **V-St**, (dc, ch 1, dc) in st or sp indicated.

PANEL (Make 3)

Ch 33 **loosely**.

Row 1 (Right side)**:** Dc in fourth ch from hook **(3 skipped chs count as first dc)** and in next 8 chs, ch 3, skip next 4 chs, work V-St in next ch, skip next ch, work V-St in next ch, ch 3, skip next 4 chs, dc in last 10 chs: 24 dc.

Note: Loop a short piece of yarn around any stitch to mark last row as **right** side and bottom edge.

Row 2: Ch 3 **(counts as first dc, now and throughout)**, turn; dc in next 8 dc, ch 3, work V-St in next ch-1 sp, ch 1, work V-St in next ch-1 sp, ch 3, skip next 2 dc, dc in last 9 dc: 22 dc.

Row 3: Ch 3, turn; dc in next 7 dc, ch 3, work V-St in next ch-1 sp, (ch 1, work V-St in next ch-1 sp) twice, ch 3, skip next 2 dc, dc in last 8 dc.

Row 4: Ch 3, turn; dc in next 6 dc, ch 3, work V-St in next ch-1 sp, ch 1, skip next ch-1 sp, (dc, ch 4, dc) in next ch-1 sp, ch 1, skip next ch-1 sp, work V-St in next ch-1 sp, ch 3, skip next 2 dc, dc in last 7 dc: 20 dc.

Row 5: Ch 3, turn; dc in next 5 dc, ch 3, work V-St in next ch-1 sp, ch 1, 10 dc in next ch-4 sp, ch 1, skip next ch-1 sp, work V-St in next ch-1 sp, ch 3, skip next 2 dc, dc in last 6 dc: 26 dc.

Row 6: Ch 3, turn; dc in next 4 dc, ch 3, work V-St in next ch-1 sp, ch 1, skip next dc, (dc in next dc, ch 1) 10 times, skip next ch-1 sp, work V-St in next ch-1 sp, ch 3, skip next 2 dc, dc in last 5 dc: 24 dc.

Row 7: Ch 3, turn; dc in next 3 dc, ch 3, work V-St in next ch-1 sp, ch 2, skip next ch-1 sp, sc in next ch-1 sp, (ch 1, sc in next ch-1 sp) 8 times, ch 2, skip next ch-1 sp, work V-St in next ch-1 sp, ch 3, skip next 2 dc, dc in last 4 dc: 12 dc.

Row 8: Ch 3, turn; dc in next 2 dc, ch 3, work V-St in next ch-1 sp, ch 2, sc in next ch-1 sp, (ch 1, sc in next ch-1 sp) 7 times, ch 2, work V-St in next ch-1 sp, ch 3, skip next 2 dc, dc in last 3 dc: 10 dc.

Row 9: Ch 3, turn; dc in next 2 dc, ch 3, work V-St in next ch-1 sp, ch 2, sc in next ch-1 sp, (ch 1, sc in next ch-1 sp) 6 times, ch 2, work V-St in next ch-1 sp, ch 3, skip next dc, dc in last 3 dc.

Row 10: Ch 3, turn; dc in next 2 dc and in next ch, ch 3, work V-St in next ch-1 sp, ch 2, sc in next ch-1 sp, (ch 1, sc in next ch-1 sp) 5 times, ch 2, work V-St in next ch-1 sp, ch 3, skip next 2 chs, dc in next ch and in last 3 dc: 12 dc.

Row 11: Ch 3, turn; dc in next 3 dc and in next ch, ch 3, work V-St in next ch-1 sp, ch 2, sc in next ch-1 sp, (ch 1, sc in next ch-1 sp) 4 times, ch 2, work V-St in next ch-1 sp, ch 3, skip next 2 chs, dc in next ch and in last 4 dc: 14 dc.

Row 12: Ch 3, turn; dc in next 4 dc and in next ch, ch 3, work V-St in next ch-1 sp, ch 2, sc in next ch-1 sp, (ch 1, sc in next ch-1 sp) 3 times, ch 2, work V-St in next ch-1 sp, ch 3, skip next 2 chs, dc in next ch and in last 5 dc: 16 dc.

Row 13: Ch 3, turn; dc in next 5 dc and in next ch, ch 3, work V-St in next ch-1 sp, ch 2, sc in next ch-1 sp, (ch 1, sc in next ch-1 sp) twice, ch 2, work V-St in next ch-1 sp, ch 3, skip next 2 chs, dc in next ch and in last 6 dc: 18 dc.

Row 14: Ch 3, turn; dc in next 6 dc and in next ch, ch 3, work V-St in next ch-1 sp, ch 2, sc in next ch-1 sp, ch 1, sc in next ch-1 sp, ch 2, work V-St in next ch-1 sp, ch 3, skip next 2 chs, dc in next ch and in last 7 dc: 20 dc.

Row 15: Ch 3, turn; dc in next 7 dc and in next ch, ch 3, work V-St in next ch-1 sp, ch 2, sc in next ch-1 sp, ch 2, work V-St in next ch-1 sp, ch 3, skip next 2 chs, dc in next ch and in last 8 dc: 22 dc.

Row 16: Ch 3, turn; dc in next 8 dc and in next ch, ch 3, work V-St in each of next 2 ch-1 sps, ch 3, skip next 2 chs, dc in next ch and in last 9 dc: 24 dc.

Row 17: Ch 3, turn; dc in next 9 dc, ch 3, work V-St in each of next 2 ch-1 sps, ch 3, dc in last 10 dc.

Rows 18-80: Repeat Rows 2-17, 3 times; then repeat Rows 2-16 once **more**.

Do **not** finish off.

PANEL EDGING

Rnd 1: Ch 1, turn; sc in first dc, ch 1, (skip next dc, sc in next dc, ch 1) 4 times, (sc, ch 1) twice in next ch-3 sp, sc in next ch-1 sp, ch 1, skip next dc, sc in sp **before** next dc, ch 1, sc in next ch-1 sp, ch 1, (sc, ch 1) twice in next ch-3 sp, skip next dc, (sc in next dc, ch 1, skip next dc) 4 times, (sc, ch 3, sc) in last dc, ch 1; working in end of rows, (sc, ch 1) evenly across; working in free loops of beginning ch ***(Fig. 29b, page 124)***, (sc, ch 3, sc) in first ch, ch 1, sc in next ch, ch 1, (skip next ch, sc in next ch, ch 1) 14 times, (sc, ch 3, sc) in next ch, ch 1; working in end of rows, (sc, ch 1) evenly across, sc in same st as first sc, ch 3; join with slip st to first sc.

Note: To work **Puff St**, (YO, insert hook in sp indicated, YO and pull up a loop even with loop on hook) twice, YO and draw through all 5 loops on hook ***(Fig. 15, page 120)***.

Rnd 2: Turn; slip st in first corner ch-3 sp, ch 2, ★ work (Puff St, ch 3, Puff St) in corner ch-3 sp, ch 1, (work Puff St in next ch-1 sp, ch 1) across to next corner ch-3 sp; repeat from ★ around; join with slip st to top of first Puff St.

Rnd 3: Ch 1, turn; sc in same st, ★ sc in each ch-1 sp and in each Puff St across to next corner ch-3 sp, 3 sc in corner ch-3 sp; repeat from ★ around; join with slip st to first sc, finish off.

ASSEMBLY

With **right** sides facing, lay out Panels with all marked edges at bottom.

Weave Panels together ***(Fig. 31, page 125)***, beginning in center sc of first corner and ending in center sc of next corner.

EDGING

With **right** side facing, join yarn with slip st in top right corner; ch 2, working from **left** to **right**, skip next sc, ★ work reverse hdc in next sc ***(Figs. 27a-d, page 123)***, ch 1, skip next sc; repeat from ★ around skipping joinings; join with slip st to base of beginning ch-2, finish off.

FIRESIDE THROW

Worked in your choice of colors, this thick, warm afghan can be completed before the embers in the fireplace fade away. It's a great project for using up your yarn scraps!

Finished Size: Approximately 45" x 60"

MATERIALS

Worsted Weight Yarn, approximately:
- Assorted colors - 73 ounces, (2,070 grams, 4,795 yards) **total**
- ***Note:*** Two rows in pattern require approximately 65 yards

Crochet hook, size P (10.00 mm) **or** size needed for gauge

Note: Entire Afghan is worked holding two strands of yarn together.

GAUGE: In pattern, 14 sts = 6" and 8 rows = $3^1/2$"

Note: Change color every 2 rows as desired.

Ch 106 **loosely**.

Row 1 (Right side)**:** Sc in second ch from hook, dc in next ch, (slip st in next ch, dc in next ch) across to last ch, sc in last ch: 105 sts.

Note: Loop a short piece of yarn around any stitch to mark last row as **right** side.

Row 2: Ch 1, turn; sc in first sc, slip st in next dc, (dc in next slip st, slip st in next dc) across to last sc, sc in last sc; finish off.

Row 3: With **right** side facing, join yarn with sc in first sc ***(see Joining With Sc, page 124)***; dc in next slip st, (slip st in next dc, dc in next slip st) across to last sc, sc in last sc.

Repeat Rows 2 and 3 until Afghan measures approximately 60" from beginning ch, ending by working Row 2.

NINE-PATCH GRANNY

Featuring granny squares that are joined as you go, this afghan is super-easy to stitch. Each block is made up of nine squares in alternating colors to create a patchwork quilt effect. Worked in rich contrasting hues, the wrap is finished with a scalloped edging.

Finished Size: Approximately 53½" x 69"

MATERIALS

Worsted Weight Yarn, approximately:
- MC (Black) - 29½ ounces, (840 grams, 1,855 yards)
- Color A (Maroon) - 17½ ounces, (500 grams, 1,100 yards)
- Color B (Tan) - 24 ounces, (680 grams, 1,510 yards)

Crochet hook, size N (9.00 mm) **or** size needed for gauge

Note: Entire Afghan is worked holding two strands of yarn together.

GAUGE: Each Square = 3¾"

FIRST SQUARE

With MC, ch 4; join with slip st to form a ring.
Rnd 1 (Right side)**:** Ch 3, 2 dc in ring, (ch 2, 3 dc in ring) 3 times, hdc in top of beginning ch-3 to form last sp: 4 sps.
Note: Loop a short piece of yarn around any stitch to mark last round as **right** side.
Rnd 2: Ch 3, (2 dc, ch 2, 3 dc) in same sp, ch 1, ★ (3 dc, ch 2, 3 dc) in next ch-2 sp, ch 1; repeat from ★ around; join with slip st to top of beginning ch-3, finish off: 8 sps.

PLACEMENT CHART

Row 1 ↓

	A	B	A		B	A	B		A	B	A	
	B	A	B		A	B	A		B	A	B	
	A	B	A		B	A	B		A	B	A	
	B	A	B		A	B	A		B	A	B	
	A	B	A		B	A	B		A	B	A	
	B	A	B		A	B	A		B	A	B	
	A	B	A		B	A	B		A	B	A	
	B	A	B		A	B	A		B	A	B	
	A	B	A		B	A	B		A	B	A	
	B	A	B		A	B	A		B	A	B	
	A	B	A		B	A	B		A	B	A	
	B	A	B		A	B	A		B	A	B	

↑ Row 2

ADDITIONAL SQUARES

Following Placement Chart, make Squares using color indicated (use MC for blank Squares).

Ch 4; join with slip st to form a ring.
Rnd 1 (Right side)**:** Ch 3, 2 dc in ring, (ch 2, 3 dc in ring) 3 times, hdc in top of beginning ch-3 to form last sp: 4 sps.
Rnd 2: Work One or Two Side Joining ***(Fig. 21, page 122)***.

ONE SIDE JOINING

Rnd 2: Ch 3, (2 dc, ch 2, 3 dc) in same sp, ch 1, (3 dc, ch 2, 3 dc) in next ch-2 sp, ch 1, 3 dc in next ch-2 sp, ch 1, holding Squares with **wrong** sides together, slip st in corner ch-2 sp on **previous Square**, ch 1, 3 dc in same ch-2 sp on **new Square**, ch 1, slip st in next ch-1 sp on **previous Square**, 3 dc in next ch-2 sp on **new Square**, ch 1, slip st in next corner ch-2 sp on **previous Square**, ch 1, 3 dc in same ch-2 sp on **new Square**, ch 1; join with slip st to top of beginning ch-3, finish off.

TWO SIDE JOINING

Rnd 2: Ch 3, (2 dc, ch 2, 3 dc) in same sp, ch 1, 3 dc in next ch-2 sp, ch 1, holding Squares with **wrong** sides together, ★ slip st in corner ch-2 sp on **previous Square**, ch 1, 3 dc in same ch-2 sp on **new Square**, ch 1, slip st in next ch-1 sp on **previous Square**, 3 dc in next ch-2 sp on **new Square**, ch 1, slip st in next corner ch-2 sp on **previous Square**, ch 1; repeat from ★ once **more**, 3 dc in same ch-2 sp on **new Square**, ch 1; join with slip st to top of beginning ch-3, finish off.

EDGING

Rnd 1: With **right** side facing, join Color B with slip st in any corner ch-2 sp; ch 3, (2 dc, ch 2, 3 dc) in same sp, ch 1, (3 dc in next sp, ch 1) across to next corner ch-2 sp, ★ (3 dc, ch 2, 3 dc) in corner ch-2 sp, ch 1, (3 dc in next sp, ch 1) across to next corner ch-2 sp; repeat from ★ around; join with slip st to top of beginning ch-3, finish off.
Rnd 2: With **right** side facing, join Color A with slip st in any corner ch-2 sp; ch 3, (2 dc, ch 2, 3 dc) in same sp, ch 1, sc in next sp, ch 1, ★ (3 dc, ch 2, 3 dc) in next sp, ch 1, sc in next sp, ch 1; repeat from ★ around; join with slip st to top of beginning ch-3, finish off.

WAVY STRIPES

Wavy ribbons in shades of rose alternate on a bed of black for this textured throw. The stripes are worked across the length of the afghan using treble and double crochet clusters. You'll be smitten by the pattern's timeless charm!

Finished Size: Approximately 46" x 60 1/2"

MATERIALS

Worsted Weight Yarn, approximately:
- Color A (Antique Rose) - 16 ounces, (450 grams, 1,190 yards)
- Color B (Dark Antique Rose) - 15 ounces, (430 grams, 1,115 yards)
- Color C (Black) - 14 1/4 ounces, (400 grams, 1,060 yards)

Crochet hook, size P (10.00 mm) **or** size needed for gauge

Note: Each row is worked across length of Afghan holding two strands of yarn together. When joining yarn and finishing off, leave an 8" length at end to be worked into fringe.

GAUGE: In pattern, 3 repeats = 10" and 8 rows = 6"

PATTERN STITCHES

DC CLUSTER

★ YO, insert hook in st indicated, YO and pull up a loop, YO and draw through 2 loops on hook; repeat from ★ once **more**, YO and draw through all 3 loops on hook ***(Figs. 16a & b, page 120)***.

TR CLUSTER

★ YO twice, insert hook in st indicated, YO and pull up a loop, (YO and draw through 2 loops on hook) twice; repeat from ★ once **more**, YO and draw through all 3 loops on hook.

With Color A, ch 146 **loosely**.

Row 1 (Right side)**:** Sc in second ch from hook, ★ ch 1, skip next ch, work dc Cluster in next ch, ch 1, skip next ch, work tr Cluster in next ch, ch 1, skip next ch, work dc Cluster in next ch, ch 1, skip next ch, sc in next ch; repeat from ★ across; finish off: 72 ch-1 sps.

Note: Loop a short piece of yarn around any stitch to mark last row as **right** side.

Row 2: With **wrong** side facing, join Color C with sc in first sc ***(see Joining With Sc, page 124)***; (ch 1, skip next ch, sc in next st) across; finish off.

Row 3: With **right** side facing, join Color B with slip st in first sc; ch 5, skip next ch, work dc Cluster in next sc, ch 1, skip next ch, sc in next sc, ch 1, skip next ch, work dc Cluster in next sc, ch 1, ★ skip next ch, work tr Cluster in next sc, ch 1, skip next ch, work dc Cluster in next sc, ch 1, skip next ch, sc in next sc, ch 1, skip next ch, work dc Cluster in next sc, ch 1; repeat from ★ across to last 2 sts, skip next ch, tr in last sc; finish off.

Row 4: With **wrong** side facing, join Color C with sc in first tr; (ch 1, skip next ch, sc in next st) across to turning ch, ch 1, skip next ch, sc in next ch; finish off.

Row 5: With **right** side facing, join Color A with sc in first sc; ★ ch 1, skip next ch, work dc Cluster in next sc, ch 1, skip next ch, work tr Cluster in next sc, ch 1, skip next ch, work dc Cluster in next sc, ch 1, skip next ch, sc in next sc; repeat from ★ across; finish off.

Repeat Rows 2-5 until Afghan measures approximately 46" from beginning ch, ending by working Row 5.

Add additional fringe to each end of **right** side rows ***(Figs. 33b & d, page 126)***, using four 18" strands of corresponding color and four 18" strands of Color C held together.

GOLDEN WAVES

Ripples of double crochet and chain stitches create a quick-to-finish blanket with harvesttime appeal. The wavy stripes bring to mind fields of golden grain.

Finished Size: Approximately 48" x 66"

MATERIALS

Worsted Weight Yarn, approximately:
- Color A (Brown) - 15 ounces, (430 grams, 985 yards)
- Color B (Dark Gold) - 13 ounces, (370 grams, 855 yards)
- Color C (Gold) - 13 ounces, (370 grams, 855 yards)
- Color D (Light Gold) - 13 ounces, (370 grams, 855 yards)

Crochet hook, size N (9.00 mm) **or** size needed for gauge

Note: Entire Afghan is worked holding two strands of yarn together.

GAUGE: 17 sts (point to point) and 6 rows = 6"

STRIPE SEQUENCE

2 Rows of **each** color: Color A ***(Fig. 30a, page 124)***, ★ Color B, Color C, Color D, Color A; repeat from ★ 7 times **more**.

Note: To work **decrease**, ★ YO, insert hook in **next** st or ch-1 sp, YO and pull up a loop, YO and draw through 2 loops on hook; repeat from ★ once **more**, YO and draw through all 3 loops on hook **(counts as one dc)**.

With Color A, ch 138 **loosely**.

Row 1: Dc in fourth ch from hook, decrease twice, ch 1, (dc in next ch, ch 1) 5 times, ★ decrease 6 times, ch 1, (dc in next ch, ch 1) 5 times; repeat from ★ across to last 6 chs, decrease 3 times: 48 ch-1 sps.

Row 2 (Right side)**:** Ch 3 **(counts as first dc, now and throughout)**, turn; dc in next dc, decrease twice, ch 1, dc in next dc, ch 1, (dc in next ch-1 sp, ch 1, dc in next dc, ch 1) twice, ★ decrease 6 times, ch 1, dc in next dc, ch 1, (dc in next ch-1 sp, ch 1, dc in next dc, ch 1) twice; repeat from ★ across to last 2 ch-1 sps, decrease 3 times, leave beginning ch unworked.

Note: Loop a short piece of yarn around any stitch to mark last row as **right** side.

Rows 3-66: Ch 3, turn; dc in next dc, decrease twice, ch 1, dc in next dc, ch 1, (dc in next ch-1 sp, ch 1, dc in next dc, ch 1) twice, ★ decrease 6 times, ch 1, dc in next dc, ch 1, (dc in next ch-1 sp, ch 1, dc in next dc, ch 1) twice; repeat from ★ across to last 2 ch-1 sps, decrease 3 times, leave last dc unworked.

Finish off.

CHRISTMAS TARTAN PLAID

Alternating rows of dark green, creamy tan, and rich cranberry give this afghan Christmasy warmth. The plaid look is achieved by vertically weaving six strands of yarn through the mesh background that's worked in chain and half double crochet stitches. For a pretty fringe, several inches of yarn are left at the ends of the woven stripes.

Finished Size: Approximately 44" x 63"

MATERIALS

Worsted Weight Yarn, approximately:
MC (Green) - 24 1/2 ounces, (700 grams, 1,540 yards)
Color A (Red) - 12 ounces, (340 grams, 755 yards)
Color B (Tan) - 8 ounces, (230 grams, 505 yards)
Crochet hook, size P (10.00 mm) **or** size needed for gauge
Yarn needle

Note: Entire Afghan is worked holding two strands of yarn together.

GAUGE: (Ch 1, dc) 5 times and 5 rows = 4"

STRIPE SEQUENCE

3 Rows MC ***(Fig. 30a, page 124)***, 1 row Color B, 3 rows MC, ★ 2 rows Color A, 1 row Color B, 2 rows Color A, 3 rows MC, 1 row Color B, 3 rows MC; repeat from ★ 5 times **more**.

With MC, ch 113 **loosely**.
Row 1 (Right side)**:** Hdc in fifth ch from hook, ★ ch 1, skip next ch, hdc in next ch; repeat from ★ across: 55 ch-sps.
Row 2: Ch 3 **(counts as first hdc plus ch 1, now and throughout)**, turn; (hdc in next hdc, ch 1) across, skip next ch, hdc in next ch: 55 ch-1 sps.
Rows 3-79: Ch 3, turn; hdc in next hdc, (ch 1, hdc in next hdc) across.
Finish off.

WEAVING

Each row is woven vertically with 6 strands of yarn.
Lay Afghan flat on a hard surface.
First Row: Thread yarn needle with six 84" strands of MC. Hold Afghan horizontally with beginning ch at lower right corner. Leaving a 7" length of yarn for fringe, insert needle down through ch below first ch-1 sp on Row 1. Bring needle up through first ch-1 sp on Row 1 and go down in adjoining ch-1 sp on Row 2. Continue weaving up and down in each ch-1 sp across. Insert needle through ch at edge of Afghan. Pull row of weaving out evenly so Afghan does not pucker. Tie a knot close to each edge of Afghan.
Next Row: With MC and alternating up and down positions with those of preceding row, weave next row in same manner.
Continue weaving in the following color sequence:
1 Row MC, 1 row Color B, 3 rows MC, ★ 2 rows Color A, 1 row Color B, 2 rows Color A, 3 rows MC, 1 row Color B, 3 rows MC; repeat from ★ 3 times **more**.

When weaving is completed, trim fringe ends evenly.

DISTINCTIVELY DOUBLE

Striking color combinations, luxuriously soft yarns, and distinctive patterns characterize the handsome afghans in this sophisticated collection. At home with all your fine furnishings, these tasteful throws are created using traditional stitches such as shells, popcorns, and puffs for rich texture. Their classic looks and enduring elegance will never go out of style!

CASCADE OF ROSES

This exquisite afghan captures the splendor of yesteryear. The sequence of colors helps the double crochet clusters evoke the look of regal rose buds and blossoms.

Finished Size: Approximately 46" x 61"

MATERIALS

Worsted Weight Yarn, approximately:
MC (Rose) - 21 1/2 ounces, (610 grams, 1,350 yards)
Color A (Teal) - 18 ounces, (510 grams, 1,130 yards)
Color B (Dark Rose) - 21 1/2 ounces, (610 grams, 1,350 yards)
Crochet hook, size N (9.00 mm) **or** size needed for gauge

Note: Entire Afghan is worked holding two strands of yarn together.

GAUGE: One repeat = 4 3/4" and 4 rows = 3"

STRIPE SEQUENCE

One row of **each** color: Color A ***(Fig. 30a, page 124)***, MC, ★ Color B, MC, Color A, MC; repeat from ★ throughout.

With Color A, ch 112 **loosely**.

Row 1: Sc in second ch from hook, ch 2, skip next ch, sc in next ch, ★ skip next 3 chs, (3 tr, ch 4, sc) in next ch, ch 2, skip next ch, (sc, ch 4, 3 tr) in next ch, skip next 3 chs, sc in next ch, ch 2, skip next ch, sc in next ch; repeat from ★ across: 19 ch-2 sps.

Note: To work **Cluster**, ★ YO, insert hook in sp indicated, YO and pull up a loop, YO and draw through 2 loops on hook; repeat from ★ once **more**, YO and draw through all 3 loops on hook ***(Figs. 16a & b, page 120)***.

Row 2 (Right side)**:** Ch 4, turn; dc in first ch-2 sp, ch 1, skip next 4 sts, sc in next ch, ch 2, work Cluster in next ch-2 sp, ch 2, skip next sc and next 3 chs, sc in next ch, ch 1, ★ (dc, ch 1) twice in next ch-2 sp, skip next 4 sts, sc in next ch, ch 2, work Cluster in next ch-2 sp, ch 2, skip next sc and next 3 chs, sc in next ch, ch 1; repeat from ★ across to last ch-2 sp, dc in last ch-2 sp, ch 1, dc in last sc: 46 sps.

Note: Loop a short piece of yarn around any stitch to mark last row as **right** side.

Row 3: Ch 1, turn; sc in first dc, ch 2, ★ skip next ch-1 sp, sc in next ch-1 sp, (3 tr, ch 4, sc) in next ch-2 sp, ch 2, (sc, ch 4, 3 tr) in next ch-2 sp, sc in next ch-1 sp, ch 2; repeat from ★ across to last dc, skip last dc and next ch, sc in next ch: 19 ch-2 sps.

Row 4: Ch 4, turn; dc in first ch-2 sp, ch 1, skip next 4 sts, sc in next ch, ch 2, work Cluster in next ch-2 sp, ch 2, skip next sc and next 3 chs, sc in next ch, ch 1, ★ (dc, ch 1) twice in next ch-2 sp, skip next 4 sts, sc in next ch, ch 2, work Cluster in next ch-2 sp, ch 2, skip next sc and next 3 chs, sc in next ch, ch 1; repeat from ★ across to last ch-2 sp, dc in last ch-2 sp, ch 1, dc in last sc: 46 sps.

Repeat Rows 3 and 4 until Afghan measures approximately 58 1/2" from beginning ch, ending by working Row 4.

Finish off.

EDGING

Rnd 1: With **right** side facing and working in free loops of beginning ch ***(Fig. 29b, page 124)***, join MC with slip st in ch at base of first sc; ch 1, 3 sc in same ch, sc in next 109 chs, 3 sc in next ch; work 145 sc evenly spaced across end of rows; 3 sc in next dc, sc in each st across to last dc, sc in last dc and in next ch, 3 sc in next ch; work 145 sc evenly spaced across end of rows; join with slip st to first sc: 520 sc.

Rnd 2: Ch 1, sc in same st and in each sc around working 3 sc in each corner; join with slip st to first sc, finish off: 528 sc.

Rnd 3: With **right** side facing, join Color B with slip st in any corner sc; ch 1, (sc, ch 2, sc) in same st, skip next sc, ★ (sc, ch 2, sc) in next sc, skip next sc; repeat from ★ around; join with slip st to first sc, finish off.

PEACHY ELEGANCE

Worked in shades of peach, lacy V-stitches and double crochets form this lush afghan for the parlor. A simple edging of double crochets provides a nice finish.

Finished Size: Approximately 46" x 64"

MATERIALS

Worsted Weight Yarn, approximately:
MC (Peach) - 34½ ounces, (980 grams, 2,365 yards)
CC (Dark Peach) - 12½ ounces, (360 grams, 855 yards)
Crochet hook, size P (10.00 mm) **or** size needed for gauge

Note: Entire Afghan is worked holding two strands of yarn together.

GAUGE: 8 dc = 4" and 5 rows = 4¾"

STRIPE SEQUENCE

5 Rows MC ***(Fig. 30a, page 124)***, ★ 1 row CC, 3 rows MC, 1 row CC, 5 rows MC; repeat from ★ 5 times **more**.

With MC, ch 91 **loosely**.

Row 1 (Right side)**:** 3 Dc in fifth ch from hook, (skip next 2 chs, 3 dc in next ch) across to last 2 chs, skip next ch, dc in last ch: 89 sts.

Note: Loop a short piece of yarn around any stitch to mark last row as **right** side.

Row 2: Ch 3 **(counts as first dc, now and throughout)**, turn; skip next dc, 3 dc in next dc, (skip next 2 dc, 3 dc in next dc) across to last 2 sts, skip last dc, dc in top of beginning ch: 89 dc.

Rows 3-5: Ch 3, turn; skip next dc, 3 dc in next dc, (skip next 2 dc, 3 dc in next dc) across to last 2 dc, skip next dc, dc in last dc.

Row 6: Ch 3, turn; dc in next dc and in each dc across.

Note: To work **V-St**, (dc, ch 1, dc) in st or sp indicated.

Row 7: Ch 3, turn; skip next dc, work V-St in next dc, (skip next 2 dc, work V-St in next dc) across to last 2 dc, skip next dc, dc in last dc: 29 ch-1 sps.

Rows 8 and 9: Ch 3, turn; work V-St in next ch-1 sp and in each ch-1 sp across to last 2 dc, skip next dc, dc in last dc.

Row 10: Ch 3, turn; dc in next dc and in each ch-1 sp and each dc across: 89 dc.

Rows 11-15: Ch 3, turn; skip next dc, 3 dc in next dc, (skip next 2 dc, 3 dc in next dc) across to last 2 dc, skip next dc, dc in last dc.

Rows 16-65: Repeat Rows 6-15, 5 times.

Finish off.

EDGING

With **right** side facing, join CC with slip st in any st; ch 3, dc evenly around working 3 dc in each corner; join with slip st to first dc, finish off.

FRINGE BENEFITS

The rewards of this unforgettable throw are twofold. Zigzags in deep shades of teal and a lavish woven-in fringe offer both soothing comfort and timeless elegance.

Finished Size: Approximately 48" x 66"

MATERIALS

Worsted Weight Yarn, approximately:
- MC (Dark Teal) - $15^1/2$ ounces, (440 grams, 1,150 yards)
- Color A (Teal) - $20^1/2$ ounces, (580 grams, 1,525 yards)
- Color B (Light Teal) - 8 ounces, (230 grams, 595 yards)

Crochet hook, size P (10.00 mm) **or** size needed for gauge
Yarn needle

Note: Entire Afghan is worked holding two strands of yarn together.

GAUGE: In pattern, 24 sts (2 repeats) = 12" and 10 rows = 11"

STRIPE SEQUENCE

2 Rows MC ***(Fig. 30a, page 124)***, 2 rows Color A, 2 rows Color B, 2 rows Color A, ★ 4 rows MC, 2 rows Color A, 2 rows Color B, 2 rows Color A; repeat from ★ throughout, ending by working 2 rows MC.

With MC, ch 106 **loosely**.

Row 1 (Wrong side)**:** Dc in fourth ch from hook **(3 skipped chs count as first dc)** and in next 4 chs, ★ skip next 2 chs, dc in next 5 chs, (dc, ch 2, dc) in next ch, dc in next 5 chs; repeat from ★ across to last 7 chs, skip next 2 chs, dc in next 4 chs, 2 dc in last ch: 96 dc.

Note: Loop a short piece of yarn around back of any stitch to mark **right** side.

Row 2: Ch 3 **(counts as first dc, now and throughout)**, turn; dc in same st and in next 4 dc, ★ skip next 2 dc, dc in next 5 dc, (dc, ch 2, dc) in next ch-2 sp, dc in next 5 dc; repeat from ★ across to last 7 dc, skip next 2 dc, dc in next 4 dc, 2 dc in last dc.

Repeat Row 2 until Afghan measures approximately 66" from beginning ch, ending by working a **wrong** side row. Finish off.

WEAVING

Each row is woven vertically with 6 strands of yarn.

Lay Afghan flat on a hard surface.

Thread yarn needle with six 90" strands of Color A. Hold Afghan horizontally, with **right** side facing and beginning ch at lower right corner. Leaving a 9" length of yarn for fringe, insert needle in sp above 2 skipped chs. Bring needle up through sp above skipped dc on Row 1 and go down in adjoining sp on next row. Continue weaving in sp of each row across length of Afghan. Pull row of weaving yarn out evenly so Afghan does not pucker.

Weave next row in same manner, working in ch-2 sps at alternate points.

Continue across width of Afghan in same manner.

Using six 20" strands of Color A, add fringe to each end of weaving ***(Figs. 33a & c, page 126)***, pulling all strands through loop.

Using nine 20" strands of Color A, add fringe to each end of first and last row.

CRISSCROSS CABLE

A crisscross cable panel is woven down the center of our classic Aran wrap. A rich array of popcorns and cables makes this an afghan that everyone will enjoy.

Finished Size: Approximately 56" x 72"

MATERIALS

Worsted Weight Yarn, approximately:
79 ounces, (2,240 grams, 5,195 yards)
Crochet hook, size P (10.00 mm) **or** size needed for gauge
Yarn needle

Note: Entire Afghan is worked holding two strands of yarn together.

PATTERN STITCHES

POPCORN

Work 5 dc in st indicated, drop loop from hook, insert hook in first dc of 5-dc group, hook dropped loop and draw through ***(Fig. 8b, page 119)***.

FRONT POST TREBLE CROCHET *(abbreviated FPtr)*

YO twice, insert hook from **front** to **back** around post of st indicated, YO and pull up a loop even with last st made (4 loops on hook) ***(Fig. 11, page 119)***, (YO and draw through 2 loops on hook) 3 times.

BACK POST TREBLE CROCHET *(abbreviated BPtr)*

YO twice, insert hook from **back** to **front** around post of st indicated, YO and pull up a loop even with last st made (4 loops on hook) ***(Fig. 13, page 120)***, (YO and draw through 2 loops on hook) 3 times.

POPCORN PANEL (Make 2)

GAUGE: Panel = 16"
In pattern, 7 rows = 5"

Ch 35 **loosely**.

Row 1: Dc in fourth ch from hook and in each ch across: 33 sts.

Row 2 (Right side)**:** Ch 3 **(counts as first dc, now and throughout)**, turn; work FPtr around next dc, dc in next 5 dc, ★ work Popcorn in next dc, dc in next 5 dc; repeat from ★ across to last 2 sts, work FPtr around next dc, dc in top of beginning ch: 4 Popcorns.

Note: Loop a short piece of yarn around any stitch to mark last row as **right** side and bottom edge.

Row 3: Ch 3, turn; work BPtr around next FPtr, dc in next dc and in each st across to last 2 sts, work BPtr around next FPtr, dc in last dc.

Row 4: Ch 3, turn; work FPtr around next BPtr, dc in next 2 dc, work Popcorn in next dc, ★ dc in next 5 dc, work Popcorn in next dc; repeat from ★ across to last 4 sts, dc in next 2 dc, work FPtr around next BPtr, dc in last dc: 5 Popcorns.

Row 5: Repeat Row 3.

Row 6: Ch 3, turn; work FPtr around next BPtr, dc in next 5 dc, ★ work Popcorn in next dc, dc in next 5 dc; repeat from ★ across to last 2 sts, work FPtr around next BPtr, dc in last dc: 4 Popcorns.

Repeat Rows 3-6 until Panel measures approximately 71" from beginning ch, ending by working a **wrong** side row. Finish off.

CROSS CABLE PANEL

GAUGE: Panel = 7"
In pattern, 7 rows = 5"

Ch 18 **loosely**.

Row 1: Dc in fourth ch from hook and in each ch across: 16 sts.

Row 2 (Right side)**:** Ch 3 **(counts as first dc, now and throughout)**, turn; work FPtr around next dc, dc in next 4 dc, work FPtr around each of next 4 dc, dc in next 4 dc, work FPtr around next dc, dc in top of beginning ch.

Note: Mark last row as **right** side and bottom edge.

Row 3: Ch 3, turn; work BPtr around next FPtr, dc in next 3 dc, skip next dc, work BPtr around each of next 2 FPtr, dc in same st as last BPtr made and in next FPtr, work BPtr around same FPtr as last dc made and around next FPtr, skip next dc, dc in next 3 dc, work BPtr around next FPtr, dc in last dc.

Row 4: Ch 3, turn; work FPtr around next BPtr, dc in next 2 dc, skip next dc, work FPtr around each of next 2 BPtr, dc in same BPtr as last FPtr made and in next 3 sts, work FPtr around same BPtr as last dc made and around next BPtr, skip next dc, dc in next 2 dc, work FPtr around next BPtr, dc in last dc.

Row 5: Ch 3, turn; work BPtr around next FPtr, dc in next dc, skip next dc, work BPtr around each of next 2 FPtr, dc in same st as last BPtr made and in next 5 sts, work BPtr around same FPtr as last dc made and around next FPtr, skip next dc, dc in next dc, work BPtr around next FPtr, dc in last dc.

Row 6: Ch 3, turn; work FPtr around next BPtr, dc in next 2 sts, work FPtr around same BPtr as last dc made and around next BPtr, skip next dc, dc in next 4 dc, skip next dc, work FPtr around each of next 2 BPtr, dc in same BPtr as last FPtr made and in next dc, work FPtr around next BPtr, dc in last dc.

Row 7: Ch 3, turn; work BPtr around next FPtr, dc in next 3 sts, work BPtr around same FPtr as last dc made and around next FPtr, skip next dc, dc in next 2 dc, skip next dc, work BPtr around each of next 2 FPtr, dc in same FPtr as last BPtr made and in next 2 dc, work BPtr around next FPtr, dc in last dc.

Row 8: Ch 3, turn; work FPtr around next BPtr, dc in next 4 sts, work FPtr around same BPtr as last dc made and around next BPtr, skip next 2 dc, work FPtr around each of next 2 BPtr, dc in same BPtr as last FPtr made and in next 3 dc, work FPtr around next BPtr, dc in last dc.

Row 9: Ch 3, turn; work BPtr around next FPtr, dc in next 4 dc, skip next 2 FPtr, work BPtr around each of next 2 FPtr, working **behind** 2 BPtr just made, work BPtr around first skipped FPtr and around next skipped FPtr, dc in next 4 dc, work BPtr around next FPtr, dc in last dc.

Row 10: Ch 3, turn; work FPtr around next BPtr, dc in next 3 dc, skip next dc, work FPtr around each of next 2 BPtr, dc in same BPtr as last FPtr made and in next BPtr, work FPtr around same BPtr as last dc made and around next BPtr, skip next dc, dc in next 3 dc, work FPtr around next BPtr, dc in last dc.

Row 11: Ch 3, turn; work BPtr around next FPtr, dc in next 2 dc, skip next dc, work BPtr around each of next 2 FPtr, dc in same FPtr as last BPtr made and in next 3 sts, work BPtr around same FPtr as last dc made and around next FPtr, skip next dc, dc in next 2 dc, work BPtr around next FPtr, dc in last dc.

Row 12: Ch 3, turn; work FPtr around next BPtr, dc in next dc, skip next dc, work FPtr around each of next 2 BPtr, dc in same BPtr as last FPtr made and in next 5 sts, work FPtr around same BPtr as last dc made and around next BPtr, skip next dc, dc in next dc, work FPtr around next BPtr, dc in last dc.

Row 13: Ch 3, turn; work BPtr around next FPtr, dc in next 2 sts, work BPtr around same FPtr as last dc made and around next FPtr, skip next dc, dc in next 4 dc, skip next dc, work BPtr around each of next 2 FPtr, dc in same FPtr as last BPtr made and in next dc, work BPtr around next FPtr, dc in last dc.

Row 14: Ch 3, turn; work FPtr around next BPtr, dc in next 3 sts, work FPtr around same BPtr as last dc made and around next BPtr, skip next dc, dc in next 2 dc, skip next dc, work FPtr around each of next 2 BPtr, dc in same BPtr as last FPtr made and in next 2 dc, work FPtr around next BPtr, dc in last dc.

Row 15: Ch 3, turn; work BPtr around next FPtr, dc in next 4 sts, work BPtr around same FPtr as last dc made and around next FPtr, skip next 2 dc, work BPtr around each of next 2 FPtr, dc in same FPtr as last BPtr made and in next 3 dc, work BPtr around next FPtr, dc in last dc.

Row 16: Ch 3, turn; work FPtr around next BPtr, dc in next 4 dc, skip next 2 BPtr, work FPtr around each of next 2 BPtr, working **behind** 2 FPtr just made, work FPtr around first skipped BPtr and around next skipped BPtr, dc in next 4 dc, work FPtr around next BPtr, dc in last dc.

Repeat Rows 3-16 until Panel measures approximately 71" from beginning ch, ending by working Row 16.
Finish off.

CABLE PANEL (Make 4)

Work same as Handsome Aran Cable Panel, page 59, until Panel measures approximately 71" from beginning ch, ending by working Row 5.
Finish off.

ASSEMBLY

With **right** sides facing and all marked edges at bottom, lay out Panels in the following order: Cable, Popcorn, Cable, Cross Cable, Cable, Popcorn, Cable.
Weave Panels together ***(Fig. 31, page 125)***.

EDGING

Rnd 1: With **right** side facing, join yarn with slip st in top **right** corner; ch 1, 3 sc in same st, work 108 sc evenly spaced across, 3 sc in next corner; work 142 sc evenly spaced across end of rows, 3 sc in next corner; working in free loops of beginning ch ***(Fig. 29b, page 124)***, work 108 sc evenly spaced across, 3 sc in next corner; work 142 sc evenly spaced across end of rows; join with slip st to first sc: 512 sc.

Rnd 2: Ch 2, do **not** turn; working from **left** to **right**, skip next sc, ★ work reverse hdc in next sc ***(Figs. 27a-d, page 123)***, ch 1, skip next sc; repeat from ★ around; join with slip st to base of beginning ch-2, finish off.

LACY TRELLIS

Rows of V-stitches and double crochets create this graceful throw resembling a lattice of ivy and lace. The lovely afghan will add a welcoming touch to a den or sitting room.

Finished Size: Approximately 46" x 64"

MATERIALS

Worsted Weight Yarn, approximately:
MC (Ecru) - 39 ounces, (1,110 grams, 2,450 yards)
CC (Green) - 10 ounces, (280 grams, 630 yards)
Crochet hook, size N (9.00 mm) **or** size needed for gauge

Note: Entire Afghan is worked holding two strands of yarn together.

GAUGE: In pattern, 7 sts = 3" and 4 rows = 3½"

STRIPE SEQUENCE

5 Rows MC ***(Fig. 30a, page 124)***, ★ 1 row CC, 5 rows MC; repeat from ★ 10 times **more**.

With MC, ch 106 **loosely**.

Row 1 (Right side)**:** Dc in fourth ch from hook **(3 skipped chs count as first dc)** and in each ch across: 104 dc.

Note #1: Loop a short piece of yarn around any stitch to mark last row as **right** side.

Note #2: To work **V-St**, (dc, ch 1, dc) in dc indicated.

Row 2: Ch 3 **(counts as first dc, now and throughout)**, turn; skip next dc, work V-St in next dc, (skip next 2 dc, work V-St in next dc) across to last 2 dc, skip next dc, dc in last dc: 34 ch-1 sps.

Row 3: Ch 3, turn; dc in next dc and in each ch-1 sp and each dc across: 104 dc.
Rows 4-71: Repeat Rows 2 and 3, 34 times.
Finish off.

EDGING

Rnd 1: With **right** side facing, join CC with slip st in first dc on Row 71; ch 1, 3 sc in same st, sc in each dc across to last dc, 3 sc in last dc; work 156 sc evenly spaced across end of rows; working in free loops of beginning ch ***(Fig. 29b, page 124)***, 3 sc in first ch, sc in next 102 chs, 3 sc in next ch; work 156 sc evenly spaced across end of rows; join with slip st to first sc: 528 sc.
Rnd 2: Ch 4, skip next sc, (slip st in next sc, ch 4, skip next sc) around; join with slip st in same st as joining, finish off.

CHECKMATE BASKETWEAVE

Worked with back and front post treble stitches, alternating patches of black and ecru give this sophisticated throw a woven look. The tailored edging is completed with a round of reverse single crochets.

Finished Size: Approximately 45" x 60"

MATERIALS

Worsted Weight Brushed Acrylic Yarn, approximately:
MC (Ecru) - 36 ounces, (1,020 grams, 2,775 yards)
CC (Black) - 19 ounces, (540 grams, 1,465 yards)
Crochet hook, size N (9.00 mm) **or** size needed for gauge

Note: Entire Afghan is worked holding two strands of yarn together.

GAUGE: In pattern, 10 sts and 7 rows = 4"

With MC, ch 112 **loosely**.
Row 1 (Right side): Dc in fourth ch from hook **(3 skipped chs count as first dc)** and in each ch across: 110 dc.
Note: Loop a short piece of yarn around any stitch to mark last row as **right** side.
Row 2: Ch 3 **(counts as first dc, now and throughout)**, turn; dc in FLO of next dc ***(Fig. 28, page 124)*** and each dc across changing to CC in last dc ***(Fig. 30a, page 124)***.
Note: To work **Front Post treble crochet *(abbreviated FPtr)***, YO twice, insert hook from **front** to **back** around post of dc in row **below** next dc, YO and pull up a loop (4 loops on hook) ***(Fig. 11, page 119)***, (YO and draw through 2 loops on hook) 3 times. Skip st behind FPtr.
Row 3: Ch 1, turn; sc in BLO of first dc, work 4 FPtr, (sc in BLO of next 4 dc, work 4 FPtr) across to last dc, sc in BLO of last dc changing to MC.
Row 4: Ch 3, turn; dc in FLO of next st and each st across.
Row 5: Ch 3, turn; dc in BLO of next dc and each dc across changing to CC in last dc.
Note: To work **Back Post treble crochet *(abbreviated BPtr)***, YO twice, insert hook from **back** to **front** around post of dc in row **below** next dc, YO and pull up a loop (4 loops on hook) ***(Fig. 13, page 120)***, (YO and draw through 2 loops on hook) 3 times. Skip st in front of BPtr.
Row 6: Ch 1, turn; sc in FLO of first 5 dc, work 4 BPtr, (sc in FLO of next 4 dc, work 4 BPtr) across to last 5 dc, sc in FLO of last 5 dc changing to MC in last sc.
Row 7: Ch 3, turn; dc in BLO of next st and each st across.
Row 8: Ch 3, turn; dc in FLO of next dc and each dc across changing to CC in last dc.
Repeat Rows 3-8 until Afghan measures approximately 59" from beginning ch, ending by working Row 4 or Row 7. Finish off.

EDGING

Rnd 1: With **right** side facing, join MC with slip st in any corner; ch 1, sc evenly around working 3 sc in each corner; join with slip st to first sc.
Rnd 2: Ch 1, do **not** turn; working from **left** to **right**, work reverse sc in each sc around (***Figs. 26a-d, page 123***); join with slip st to first st, finish off.

LUXURIOUS WRAP

Wrap yourself in luxury with this tasteful throw worked in shells and V-stitches. A picot edging adds an elegant touch.

Finished Size: Approximately 46" x 62"

MATERIALS

Worsted Weight Brushed Acrylic Yarn, approximately:
44 ounces, (1,250 grams, 3,395 yards)
Crochet hook, size N (9.00 mm) **or** size needed for gauge

Note: Entire Afghan is worked holding two strands of yarn together.

GAUGE: Sc, (ch 1, Shell, ch 1, sc) twice and 8 rows = 5"

PATTERN STITCHES

SHELL
5 Dc in st or sp indicated.

V-ST
(Dc, ch 1, dc) in next sc.

Ch 106 **loosely**.

Row 1 (Right side)**:** 2 Dc in fourth ch from hook **(3 skipped chs count as first dc)**, ch 1, skip next 2 chs, sc in next ch, ch 1, ★ skip next 2 chs, work Shell in next ch, ch 1, skip next 2 chs, sc in next ch, ch 1; repeat from ★ across to last 3 chs, skip next 2 chs, 3 dc in last ch: 16 Shells.

Note: Loop a short piece of yarn around any stitch to mark last row as **right** side.

Row 2: Ch 1, turn; sc in first dc, ch 1, work V-St, ch 1, ★ sc in center dc of next Shell, ch 1, work V-St, ch 1; repeat from ★ across to last 3 dc, skip next 2 dc, sc in last dc: 17 V-Sts.

Row 3: Ch 1, turn; sc in first sc, ★ ch 1, work Shell in next V-St (ch-1 sp), ch 1, sc in next sc; repeat from ★ across: 17 Shells.

Row 4: Ch 3 **(counts as first dc, now and throughout)**, turn; dc in same st, ch 1, sc in center dc of next Shell, ch 1, ★ work V-St, ch 1, sc in center dc of next Shell, ch 1; repeat from ★ across to last sc, 2 dc in last sc: 16 V-Sts.

Row 5: Ch 3, turn; 2 dc in same st, ch 1, sc in next sc, ch 1, ★ work Shell in next V-St, ch 1, sc in next sc, ch 1; repeat from ★ across to last 2 dc, skip next dc, 3 dc in last dc: 16 Shells.

Repeat Rows 2-5 until Afghan measures approximately 59" from beginning ch, ending by working Row 2; do **not** finish off.

EDGING

Rnd 1: Ch 1, turn; 2 sc in first sc, work 107 sc evenly spaced across to last sc, 3 sc in last sc; work 147 sc evenly spaced across end of rows; working in free loops of beginning ch ***(Fig. 29b, page 124)***, 3 sc in first ch, sc in next 9 chs, 2 sc in next ch, (sc in next 20 chs, 2 sc in next ch) 4 times, sc in next 8 chs, 3 sc in next ch; work 147 sc evenly spaced across end of rows, sc in same st as first sc; join with slip st to first sc: 520 sc.

Rnd 2: Ch 1, turn; (sc, ch 3) twice in same st as joining, skip next sc, (sc in next sc, ch 3, skip next sc) across to next corner sc, ★ (sc, ch 3) twice in corner sc, skip next sc, (sc in next sc, ch 3, skip next sc) across to next corner sc; repeat from ★ around; join with slip st to first sc.

Note: To work **Picot**, ch 3, slip st in third ch from hook.

Rnd 3: Turn; slip st in first ch-3 sp, ch 1, sc in same sp, work Picot, ★ (sc in next ch-3 sp, work Picot) across to next corner ch-3 sp, (sc, work Picot) twice in corner ch-3 sp; repeat from ★ around; join with slip st to first sc, finish off.

RESPLENDENT BEAUTY

For powder-puff softness, this resplendent afghan features alternating clusters and open spaces worked in rich red brushed acrylic yarn. It's beautifully finished with a border of more plush puff stitches and a picot edging.

Finished Size: Approximately 45" x 62"

MATERIALS

Worsted Weight Brushed Acrylic Yarn, approximately: 37 ounces, (1,050 grams, 2,855 yards)
Crochet hook, size P (10.00 mm) **or** size needed for gauge

Note: Entire Afghan is worked holding two strands of yarn together.

GAUGE: Hdc, (ch 1, hdc) 4 times = 4 1/2"
and 8 rows = 5 1/2"

Ch 70 **loosely**.

Row 1 (Right side)**:** Hdc in sixth ch from hook, ★ ch 1, skip next ch, hdc in next ch; repeat from ★ across: 33 ch-sps.

Note #1: Loop a short piece of yarn around any stitch to mark last row as **right** side.

Note#2: To work **Puff St**, ★ YO, insert hook in st or ch-1 sp indicated, YO and pull up a loop; repeat from ★ 3 times **more**, YO and draw through all 9 loops on hook ***(Fig. 15, page 120)***.

Row 2: Ch 2 **(counts as first hdc, now and throughout)**, turn; ★ hdc in next ch-1 sp, ch 1, work Puff St in next ch-1 sp, ch 1; repeat from ★ across to last hdc, skip last hdc, hdc in next 2 chs: 16 Puff Sts.

Row 3: Ch 3 **(counts as first hdc plus ch 1, now and throughout)**, turn; ★ hdc in next ch-1 sp, ch 1; repeat from ★ across to last 2 hdc, skip next hdc, hdc in last hdc: 33 ch-1 sps.

Row 4: Ch 2, turn; work Puff St in next ch-1 sp, ★ ch 1, hdc in next ch-1 sp, ch 1, work Puff St in next ch-1 sp; repeat from ★ across to last hdc, hdc in last hdc: 17 Puff Sts.

Row 5: Ch 3, turn; ★ hdc in next ch-1 sp, ch 1; repeat from ★ across to last hdc, hdc in last hdc: 33 ch-1 sps.

Row 6: Ch 2, turn; hdc in next ch-1 sp, ★ ch 1, work Puff St in next ch-1 sp, ch 1, hdc in next ch-1 sp; repeat from ★ across to last hdc, hdc in last hdc: 16 Puff Sts.

Repeat Rows 3-6 until Afghan measures approximately 50" from beginning ch, ending by working Row 3; do **not** finish off.

EDGING

Rnd 1: Ch 1, do **not** turn; work 97 sc evenly spaced across end of rows; working in free loops of beginning ch ***(Fig. 29b, page 124)***, sc in first 67 chs; work 97 sc evenly spaced across end of rows; sc in each st and in each ch-1 sp across; join with slip st to first sc: 328 sc.

Rnd 2: Ch 3, dc in next 96 sc, 3 dc in next sc, dc in next 65 sc, 3 dc in next sc, dc in next 97 sc, 3 dc in next sc, dc in next 65 sc, 3 dc in last sc; join with slip st to top of beginning ch-3: 336 sts.

Rnd 3: Ch 3, skip next dc, work Puff St in next dc, ch 1, ★ skip next dc, hdc in next dc, (ch 1, skip next dc, work Puff St in next dc, ch 1, skip next dc, hdc in next dc) across to next corner 3-dc group, ch 1, skip next dc, work Puff St in next dc, ch 1, (hdc in same st, ch 1) twice, work Puff St in same st, ch 1; repeat from ★ around; join with slip st to first hdc: 88 Puff Sts.

Rnd 4: Slip st in next ch-1 sp, ch 3, ★ (hdc in next ch-1 sp, ch 1) across to next corner ch-1 sp, (hdc, ch 1) twice in corner ch-1 sp; repeat from ★ 3 times **more**, (hdc in next ch-1 sp, ch 1) twice; join with slip st to first hdc.

Rnd 5: Slip st in next ch-1 sp, ch 3, work Puff St in next ch-1 sp, ch 1, ★ (hdc in next ch-1 sp, ch 1, work Puff St in next ch-1 sp, ch 1) across to next corner ch-1 sp, (hdc, ch 1) twice in corner ch-1 sp, work Puff St in next ch-1 sp, ch 1; repeat from ★ 3 times **more**, hdc in next ch-1 sp, ch 1, work Puff St in next ch-1 sp, ch 1; join with slip st to first hdc: 92 Puff Sts.

Rnd 6: Slip st in next ch-1 sp, ch 3, ★ (hdc in next ch-1 sp, ch 1) across to next corner ch-1 sp, (hdc, ch 1) twice in corner ch-1 sp; repeat from ★ 3 times **more**, (hdc in next ch-1 sp, ch 1) 4 times; join with slip st to first hdc.

Rnd 7: Slip st in next ch-1 sp, ch 3, work Puff St in next ch-1 sp, ch 1, ★ (hdc in next ch-1 sp, ch 1, work Puff St in next ch-1 sp, ch 1) across to next corner ch-1 sp, (hdc, ch 1) twice in corner ch-1 sp, work Puff St in next ch-1 sp, ch 1; repeat from ★ 3 times **more**, (hdc in next ch-1 sp, ch 1, work Puff St in next ch-1 sp, ch 1) twice; join with slip st to first hdc: 96 Puff Sts.

Note: To work **Picot**, ch 3, slip st in third ch from hook.

Rnd 8: Slip st in next ch-1 sp, ch 1, (sc, work Picot, sc) in same sp and in each sp around; join with slip st to first sc, finish off.

DISCRIMINATING TASTE

For those with a taste for both style and comfort, this pretty afghan is a winning choice. A variation of the traditional ripple pattern, the V-shaped stripes are worked in soft, tranquil colors and accented with long and extended long double crochets.

Finished Size: Approximately 52" x 69"

MATERIALS

Worsted Weight Yarn, approximately:
- Color A (Ecru) - 31½ ounces, (890 grams, 1,260 yards)
- Color B (Green) - 30 ounces, (850 grams, 1,200 yards)
- Color C (Peach) - 30 ounces, (850 grams, 1,200 yards)

Crochet hook, size P (10.00 mm) **or** size needed for gauge

Note: Entire Afghan is worked holding two strands of yarn together.

GAUGE: 37 sts (point to point) = 13" and 8 rows = 5"

STRIPE SEQUENCE

4 Rows of **each** color: ★ Color A ***(Fig. 30a, page 124)***, Color B, Color C; repeat from ★ throughout, ending by working 2 rows of Color A.

PATTERN STITCHES

LONG DOUBLE CROCHET
(abbreviated Ldc)

YO, insert hook in next st 2 rows **below**, YO and pull up a loop even with last st made, (YO and draw through 2 loops on hook) twice ***(Fig. 14a, page 120)***.

EXTENDED LONG DOUBLE CROCHET
(abbreviated ex Ldc)

YO, insert hook in next st 3 rows **below**, YO and pull up a loop even with last st made, (YO and draw through 2 loops on hook) twice.

With Color A, ch 147 **loosely**.

Row 1 (Wrong side)**:** Sc in second ch from hook and in next 16 chs, 3 sc in next ch, sc in next 17 chs, ★ skip next 2 chs, sc in next 17 chs, 3 sc in next ch, sc in next 17 chs; repeat from ★ across: 148 sc.

Note: Loop a short piece of yarn around back of any stitch to mark **right** side.

Rows 2-4: Ch 1, turn; skip first sc, sc in next 17 sc, 3 sc in next sc, ★ sc in next 17 sc, skip next 2 sc, sc in next 17 sc, 3 sc in next sc; repeat from ★ 2 times **more**, sc in next 16 sc, skip next sc, sc in last sc.

Row 5: Ch 1, turn; skip first sc, sc in next 2 sc, work Ldc, (sc in next sc, work ex Ldc, sc in next sc, work Ldc) 3 times, sc in next 2 sc, 3 sc in next sc, sc in next 2 sc, work Ldc, sc in next sc, (work ex Ldc, sc in next sc, work Ldc, sc in next sc) 3 times, ★ work ex Ldc, skip next 2 sc, work ex Ldc, sc in next sc, work Ldc, (sc in next sc, work ex Ldc, sc in next sc, work Ldc) 3 times, sc in next 2 sc, 3 sc in next sc, sc in next 2 sc, work Ldc, sc in next sc, (work ex Ldc, sc in next sc, work Ldc, sc in next sc) 3 times; repeat from ★ across to last 2 sc, skip next sc, sc in last sc.

Rows 6-8: Ch 1, turn; skip first sc, sc in next 17 sts, 3 sc in next sc, ★ sc in next 17 sts, skip next 2 sts, sc in next 17 sts, 3 sc in next sc; repeat from ★ 2 times **more**, sc in next 16 sts, skip next sc, sc in last sc.

Rows 9-110: Repeat Rows 5-8, 25 times; then repeat Rows 5 and 6 once **more**.

Finish off.

HANDSOME ARAN

The traditional lines and handsome look of this fisherman afghan are sure to be enjoyed for years to come. Featuring panels of popcorns, bobbles, and cables, the textured throw is enhanced with an edging of reverse half double crochets.

Finished Size: Approximately 45" x 62"

MATERIALS

Worsted Weight Yarn, approximately:
62 ounces, (1,760 grams, 4,075 yards)
Crochet hook, size P (10.00 mm) **or** size needed for gauge
Yarn needle

Note: Entire Afghan is worked holding two strands of yarn together.

PATTERN STITCHES

POPCORN

Work 4 dc in st indicated, drop loop from hook, insert hook in first dc of 4-dc group, hook dropped loop and draw through ***(Fig. 8a, page 119)***.

SHELL

(2 Dc, ch 2, 2 dc) in st or sp indicated.

FRONT POST DOUBLE CROCHET *(abbreviated FPdc)*

YO, insert hook from **front** to **back** around post of st indicated, YO and pull up a loop even with last st made (3 loops on hook) ***(Fig. 10, page 119)***, (YO and draw through 2 loops on hook) twice. Skip st behind FPdc.

BACK POST DOUBLE CROCHET *(abbreviated BPdc)*

YO, insert hook from **back** to **front** around post of st indicated, YO and pull up a loop even with last st made (3 loops on hook) ***(Fig. 12, page 119)***, (YO and draw through 2 loops on hook) twice. Skip st in front of BPdc.

FRONT POST TREBLE CROCHET *(abbreviated FPtr)*

YO twice, insert hook from **front** to **back** around post of st indicated, YO and pull up a loop even with last st made (4 loops on hook) ***(Fig. 11, page 119)***, (YO and draw through 2 loops on hook) 3 times. Skip st behind FPtr.

BACK POST TREBLE CROCHET *(abbreviated BPtr)*

YO twice, insert hook from **back** to **front** around post of st indicated, YO and pull up a loop even with last st made (4 loops on hook) ***(Fig. 13, page 120)***, (YO and draw through 2 loops on hook) 3 times. Skip st in front of BPtr.

POPCORN PANEL

GAUGE: Panel = 8"
In pattern, 8 rows = 5 1/2"

Ch 23 **loosely**.

Row 1: Dc in fourth ch from hook, † skip next 2 chs, work Shell in next ch, skip next 2 chs †, dc in next 7 chs, repeat from † to † once, dc in last 2 chs: 19 sts.

Row 2 (Right side)**:** Ch 3 **(counts as first dc, now and throughout)**, turn; † work FPtr around next dc, ch 2, (sc, ch 3, sc) in next ch-2 sp, ch 2, skip next 2 dc, work FPtr around next dc †, dc in next 2 dc, work Popcorn in next dc, dc in next 2 dc, repeat from † to † once, dc in top of beginning ch.

Note: Loop a short piece of yarn around any stitch to mark last row as **right** side and bottom edge.

Row 3: Ch 3, turn; † work BPtr around next FPtr, work Shell in next ch-3 sp, work BPtr around next FPtr †, dc in next 5 sts, repeat from † to † once, dc in last dc.

Row 4: Ch 3, turn; † work FPtr around next BPtr, ch 2, (sc, ch 3, sc) in next ch-2 sp, ch 2, work FPtr around next BPtr †, dc in next 2 dc, work Popcorn in next dc, dc in next 2 dc, repeat from † to † once, dc in last dc.

Repeat Rows 3 and 4 until Panel measures approximately 61" from beginning ch, ending by working Row 4.

Last Row: Ch 2, turn; † work BPtr around next FPtr, hdc in next sc and in next ch-3 sp, hdc in next sc, work BPtr around next FPtr †, hdc in next 5 sts, repeat from † to † once, hdc in last dc; finish off.

BOBBLE PANEL (Make 2)

GAUGE: Panel = 10"
In pattern, 10 rows = 5 1/2"

Ch 25 **loosely**.

Row 1 (Right side)**:** Dc in fourth ch from hook and in each ch across: 23 sts.

Note #1: Mark last row as **right** side and bottom edge.

Note #2: Push tr to back of work throughout.

Row 2: Ch 3 **(counts as first dc, now and throughout)**, turn; work BPdc around next dc, sc in next dc, (tr in next dc, sc in next dc) across to last 2 sts, work BPdc around next dc, dc in top of beginning ch.

Row 3: Ch 3, turn; work FPdc around next BPdc, sc in next sc, (tr in next tr, sc in next sc) across to last 2 sts, work FPdc around next BPdc, dc in last dc.

Row 4: Ch 3, turn; work BPdc around next FPdc, tr in next sc, (sc in next tr, tr in next sc) across to last 2 sts, work BPdc around next FPdc, dc in last dc.

Row 5: Ch 3, turn; work FPdc around next BPdc, tr in next tr, (sc in next sc, tr in next tr) across to last 2 sts, work FPdc around next BPdc, dc in last dc.
Row 6: Ch 3, turn; work BPdc around next FPdc, tr in next tr, (sc in next sc, tr in next tr) across to last 2 sts, work BPdc around next FPdc, dc in last dc.
Row 7: Ch 3, turn; work FPdc around next BPdc, sc in next tr, (tr in next sc, sc in next tr) across to last 2 sts, work FPdc around next BPdc, dc in last dc.
Row 8: Ch 3, turn; work BPdc around next FPdc, sc in next sc, (tr in next tr, sc in next sc) across to last 2 sts, work BPdc around next FPdc, dc in last dc.
Repeat Rows 3-8 until Panel measures approximately 61" from beginning ch, ending by working Row 8.
Last Row: Ch 2, turn; work FPdc around next BPdc, hdc in each st across to last 2 sts, work FPdc around next BPdc, hdc in last dc; finish off.

CABLE PANEL (Make 4)

GAUGE: Panel = 4"
In pattern, 6 rows = 5"

Ch 11 **loosely**.
Row 1 (Right side)**:** Dc in fourth ch from hook and in each ch across: 9 sts.
Note: Mark last row as **right** side and bottom edge.
Row 2: Ch 3 **(counts as first dc, now and throughout)**, turn; work BPtr around next dc, dc in next 5 dc, work BPtr around next dc, dc in top of beginning ch.
Note: To work **Cable**, ch 5 **loosely**, slip st from **front** to **back** around post of dc 2 rows **below** dc just worked (***Fig. 18a, page 121***), hdc in top loop of each ch just worked (***Fig. 18b, page 121***).
Row 3: Ch 3, turn; work FPtr around next BPtr, dc in next 3 dc, work Cable, dc in next 2 dc, work FPtr around next BPtr, dc in last dc.

Row 4: Ch 3, turn; work BPtr around next FPtr, dc in next 2 dc, skip next Cable, dc in next 3 dc, work BPtr around next FPtr, dc in last dc.
Row 5: Ch 3, turn; work FPtr around next BPtr, dc in next 3 dc, work Cable around dc to **right** of previous Cable ***(Fig. 19, page 121)***, dc in next 2 dc, work FPtr around next BPtr, dc in last dc.
Repeat Rows 4 and 5 until Panel measures approximately 61" from beginning ch, ending by working Row 5.
Finish off.

ASSEMBLY

With **right** sides facing and all marked edges at bottom, lay out Panels in the following order: Cable, Bobble, Cable, Popcorn, Cable, Bobble, Cable.
Weave Panels together ***(Fig. 31, page 125)***.

EDGING

Rnd 1: With **right** side facing, join yarn with slip st in top right corner; ch 1, 3 sc in same st, work 84 sc evenly spaced across, 3 sc in next corner; work 122 sc evenly spaced across end of rows, 3 sc in next corner; working in free loops of beginning ch ***(Fig. 29b, page 124)***, work 84 sc evenly spaced across, 3 sc in next corner; work 122 sc evenly spaced across end of rows; join with slip st to first sc: 424 sc.
Rnd 2: Ch 2, do **not** turn; working from **left** to **right**, skip next sc, ★ work reverse hdc in next sc ***(Figs. 27a-d, page 123)***, ch 1, skip next sc; repeat from ★ around; join with slip st to base of beginning ch-2, finish off.

SERENE RIPPLES

Crocheted in relaxing shades of blue and creamy white, this classic afghan invites you to cuddle up for an afternoon of reading or daydreaming. The soothing ripple pattern is worked using one strand each of variegated and solid-color yarn.

Finished Size: Approximately 48" x 64"

MATERIALS

Worsted Weight Yarn, approximately:
MC (Off-White) - 30 ounces, (850 grams, 1,710 yards)
CC (Variegated) - 30 ounces, (850 grams, 1,710 yards)
Crochet hook, size N (9.00 mm) **or** size needed for gauge

Note: Entire Afghan is worked holding one strand of MC and one strand of CC yarn together.

GAUGE: 10 dc and 5 rows = 4"

Ch 123 **loosely**.
Row 1 (Right side)**:** Dc in fourth ch from hook **(3 skipped chs count as first dc)** and in next 3 chs, ★ skip next 2 chs, dc in next 4 chs, ch 2, dc in next 4 chs; repeat from ★ across to last 6 chs, skip next 2 chs, dc in next 3 chs, 2 dc in last ch: 98 dc.
Note: Loop a short piece of yarn around any stitch to mark last row as **right** side.
Row 2: Ch 3 **(counts as first dc)**, turn; dc in same st and in next 3 dc, skip next 2 dc, dc in next 3 dc, ★ (dc, ch 2, dc) in next ch-2 sp, dc in next 3 dc, skip next 2 dc, dc in next 3 dc; repeat from ★ across to last dc, 2 dc in last dc.
Repeat Row 2 until Afghan measures approximately 64" from beginning ch, ending by working a **right** side row.
Finish off.

DISTINCTIVE DIAMONDS

Puff stitches form distinctive diamonds when the blocks of this afghan are sewn together. Jumbo cross stitches at the intersections help continue the diagonal lines.

Finished Size: Approximately 50" x 68"

MATERIALS

Worsted Weight Brushed Acrylic Yarn, approximately:
52 ounces, (1,480 grams, 4,010 yards)
Crochet hook, size N (9.00 mm) **or** size needed for gauge
Yarn needle

Note: Entire Afghan is worked holding two strands of yarn together.

GAUGE: Each Square = 9 1/4"

Note: To work **Puff St**, ★ YO, insert hook in sp indicated, YO and draw up a loop; repeat from ★ 3 times **more**, YO and draw through all 9 loops on hook ***(Fig. 15, page 120)***.

SQUARE (Make 35)

Ch 6; join with slip st to form a ring.

Rnd 1: Ch 1, ★ work Puff St in ring, ch 4, work Puff St in ring, ch 1; repeat from ★ 3 times **more**; join with slip st to top of first Puff St: 8 Puff Sts.

Rnd 2: Ch 3 **(counts as first dc, now and throughout)**, work (Puff St, ch 5, Puff St) in next ch-4 sp, ch 1, dc in next Puff St and in next ch, ★ dc in next Puff St, work (Puff St, ch 5, Puff St) in next ch-4 sp, ch 1, dc in next Puff St and in next ch; repeat from ★ around; join with slip st to first dc: 12 dc.

Rnd 3: Ch 3, dc in next Puff St, work (Puff St, ch 5, Puff St) in next loop, ch 1, dc in next Puff St and in next ch, ★ dc in next 3 dc and in next Puff St, work (Puff St, ch 5, Puff St) in next loop, ch 1, dc in next Puff St and in next ch; repeat from ★ 2 times **more**, dc in last 2 dc; join with slip st to first dc: 24 dc.

Rnd 4: Ch 3, dc in next 2 sts, work (Puff St, ch 5, Puff St) in next loop, ch 1, dc in next Puff St and in next ch, ★ dc in next 7 sts, work (Puff St, ch 5, Puff St) in next loop, ch 1, dc in next Puff St and in next ch; repeat from ★ 2 times **more**, dc in last 4 dc; join with slip st to first dc: 36 dc.

Rnd 5: Ch 3, dc in next 3 sts, work (Puff St, ch 5, Puff St) in next loop, ch 1, dc in next Puff St and in next ch, ★ dc in next 10 sts, work (Puff St, ch 5, Puff St) in next loop, ch 1, dc in next Puff St and in next ch; repeat from ★ 2 times **more**, dc in last 6 dc; join with slip st to first dc, finish off: 48 dc.

ASSEMBLY

Whipstitch Squares together ***(Fig. 32b, page 125)*** forming 5 vertical strips of 7 Squares each, beginning in center ch of first corner and ending in center ch of next corner; then whipstitch strips together in same manner.

EDGING

Rnd 1: With **right** side facing, join yarn with slip st in any corner loop; ch 3, (2 dc, ch 3, 4 dc) in same loop, dc in next ch and in next 12 dc, dc in next Puff St and in next ch, (2 dc in next loop, dc in joining, 3 dc in next loop, dc in next ch and in next 12 dc, dc in next Puff St and in next ch) across to next corner loop, ★ (3 dc, ch 3, 4 dc) in corner loop, dc in next ch and in next 12 dc, dc in next Puff St and in next ch, (2 dc in next loop, dc in joining, 3 dc in next loop, dc in next ch and in next 12 dc, dc in next Puff St and in next ch) across to next corner loop; repeat from ★ around; join with slip st to first dc.

Rnd 2: Ch 3, dc in next 2 dc and in next ch, 3 dc in next ch, ★ dc in next ch and in each dc and ch across to center ch of next corner, 3 dc in center ch; repeat from ★ 2 times **more**, dc in next ch and in each dc across; join with slip st to first dc, finish off.

CROSS STITCH

Cross stitches are worked at each intersection of 4 Squares. Thread a needle with a 24" double strand of yarn. Holding Afghan with **right** side facing and short edge at top, bring needle up from back of work through corner loop of first Square, leaving a 3" end on back. Work over this end to secure. Bring needle down through corner loop of Square diagonally across, pulling stitch flat against fabric, but not so tight as to pucker the fabric (one half of a cross stitch made). Work over same half cross stitch 4 times **more**. Bring needle up through corner loop of third Square, then down through corner loop of fourth Square. Repeat second half of cross stitch 4 times **more** ***(Fig. 1)***; secure end.

Fig. 1

CONTRASTING INTEREST

Patterned stripes of turquoise create a dramatic contrast against the black background of this handsome afghan. The throw, which is worked in single and double crochets, will add interest to the study or den.

Finished Size: Approximately 45" x 68"

MATERIALS

Worsted Weight Yarn, approximately:
MC (Black) - 33 ounces, (940 grams, 2,320 yards)
CC (Aqua) - 18 ounces, (510 grams, 1,265 yards)
Crochet hook, size P (10.00 mm) **or** size needed for gauge

Note: Entire Afghan is worked holding two strands of yarn together.

GAUGE: In pattern, 7 sts = 3" and 10 rows = $4^{1}/_{2}$"

With MC, ch 104 **loosely**.
Row 1 (Right side)**:** Sc in second ch from hook, ★ ch 1, skip next ch, sc in next ch; repeat from ★ across: 52 sc.
Note: Loop a short piece of yarn around any stitch to mark last row as **right** side.
Row 2: Ch 1, turn; sc in first sc, ★ ch 1, skip next ch, sc in next sc; repeat from ★ across; finish off.
Row 3: With **right** side facing, join CC with sc in first sc ***(see Joining With Sc, page 124)***; working in **front** of next ch, dc in ch-1 sp one row **below**, sc in next sc, ★ ch 1, skip next ch, sc in next sc, working in **front** of next ch, dc in ch-1 sp one row **below**, sc in next sc; repeat from ★ across; finish off: 26 dc.
Row 4: With **wrong** side facing, join MC with sc in first sc; ★ ch 1, skip next st, sc in next sc; repeat from ★ across; finish off.
Row 5: With **right** side facing, join CC with sc in first sc; ch 1, skip next ch, sc in next sc, ★ working in **front** of next ch, dc in ch-1 sp one row **below**, sc in next sc, ch 1, skip next ch, sc in next sc; repeat from ★ across: 25 dc.
Row 6: Ch 1, turn; sc in first sc, ★ ch 1, skip next st, sc in next sc; repeat from ★ across; finish off.
Row 7: With **right** side facing, join MC with sc in first sc; ch 1, skip next ch, sc in next sc, ★ working in **front** of next ch, dc in dc one row **below**, sc in next sc, ch 1, skip next ch, sc in next sc; repeat from ★ across.
Row 8: Ch 1, turn; sc in first sc, ★ ch 1, skip next st, sc in next sc; repeat from ★ across; finish off.
Row 9: With **right** side facing, join CC with sc in first sc; ch 1, skip next ch, sc in next sc, ★ working in **front** of next ch, dc in dc one row **below**, sc in next sc, ch 1, skip next ch, sc in next sc; repeat from ★ across; finish off.
Row 10: With **wrong** side facing, join MC with sc in first sc; ★ ch 1, skip next st, sc in next sc; repeat from ★ across; finish off.
Row 11: With **right** side facing, join CC with sc in first sc; working in **front** of next ch, dc in ch-1 sp one row **below**, sc in next sc, ★ ch 1, skip next ch, sc in next sc, working in **front** of next ch, dc in ch-1 sp one row **below**, sc in next sc; repeat from ★ across: 26 dc.
Row 12: Ch 1, turn; sc in first sc, ★ ch 1, skip next st, sc in next sc; repeat from ★ across; finish off.
Row 13: With **right** side facing, join MC with sc in first sc; working in **front** of next ch, dc in dc one row **below**, sc in next sc, ★ ch 1, skip next ch, sc in next sc, working in **front** of next ch, dc in dc one row **below**, sc in next sc; repeat from ★ across.
Row 14: Ch 1, turn; sc in first sc, ★ ch 1, skip next st, sc in next sc; repeat from ★ across; finish off.
Row 15: With **right** side facing, join CC with sc in first sc; working in **front** of next ch, dc in dc one row **below**, sc in next sc, ★ ch 1, skip next ch, sc in next sc, working in **front** of next ch, dc in dc one row **below**, sc in next sc; repeat from ★ across; finish off.
Rows 16-19: Repeat Rows 4-7.
Row 20: Ch 1, turn; sc in first sc, ★ ch 1, skip next st, sc in next sc; repeat from ★ across.
Row 21: Ch 1, turn; sc in first sc, working in **front** of next ch, dc in ch-1 sp one row **below**, sc in next sc, ★ ch 1, skip next ch, sc in next sc, working in **front** of next ch, dc in ch-1 sp one row **below**, sc in next sc; repeat from ★ across: 26 dc.
Row 22: Ch 1, turn; sc in first sc, ★ ch 1, skip next st, sc in next sc; repeat from ★ across.
Row 23: Ch 1, turn; sc in first sc, ch 1, skip next ch, sc in next sc, ★ working in **front** of next ch, dc in ch-1 sp one row **below**, sc in next sc, ch 1, skip next ch, sc in next sc; repeat from ★ across: 25 dc.
Rows 24-27: Repeat Rows 20-23.
Row 28: Ch 1, turn; sc in first sc, ★ ch 1, skip next st, sc in next sc; repeat from ★ across; finish off.
Rows 29-150: Repeat Rows 3-28, 4 times; then repeat Rows 3-20 once **more**; do **not** finish off.

EDGING

Rnd 1: Ch 1, turn; sc in first sc, ch 1, skip next ch, (sc in next sc, ch 1, skip next ch) across to last sc, (sc, ch 2, sc) in last sc, ch 1; working in end of rows, skip first row, sc in next row, ch 1, (skip next row, sc in next row, ch 1) across; working in free loops of beginning ch ***(Fig. 29b, page 124)***, (sc, ch 2, sc) in first ch, ch 1, skip next ch, (sc in next ch, ch 1, skip next ch) 50 times, (sc, ch 2, sc) in next ch, ch 1; working in end of rows, skip first row, sc in next row, ch 1, (skip next row, sc in next row, ch 1) across, sc in same sc as first sc, ch 2; join with slip st to first sc: 258 sps.

Rnd 2: Slip st in first ch-1 sp, ★ ch 1, (slip st in next ch-1 sp, ch 1) across to next corner ch-2 sp, (slip st, ch 1) twice in corner ch-2 sp; repeat from ★ around; join with slip st to first st, finish off.

BOLD HERITAGE

With its striking squares of classic blue and white, this afghan will be a bold addition to your decor. The simple motifs are a breeze to assemble and whipstitch together to form this eye-catching throw.

Finished Size: Approximately 42" x 63"

MATERIALS

Worsted Weight Yarn, approximately:
MC (Blue) - 18 ounces, (510 grams, 1,185 yards)
CC (White) - 31½ ounces, (890 grams, 2,070 yards)
Crochet hook, size N (9.00 mm) **or** size needed for gauge
Yarn needle

Note: Entire Afghan is worked holding two strands of yarn together.

GAUGE: Each Square = 10½"

SQUARE (Make 24)

Rnd 1 (Right side)**:** With MC, ch 4, 2 dc in fourth ch from hook, ch 2, (3 dc in same ch, ch 2) 3 times; join with slip st to top of beginning ch-4: 4 ch-2 sps.

Note: Loop a short piece of yarn around any stitch to mark last round as **right** side.

Rnd 2: Ch 4, skip next dc, dc in next dc, ch 1, (dc, ch 2, dc) in next ch-2 sp, ch 1, ★ dc in next dc, ch 1, skip next dc, dc in next dc, ch 1, (dc, ch 2, dc) in next ch-2 sp, ch 1; repeat from ★ around; join with slip st to third ch of beginning ch-4: 16 sps.

Rnd 3: Ch 4, dc in next dc, ch 1, dc in next dc, (2 dc, ch 1, 2 dc) in next ch-2 sp, dc in next dc, ★ (ch 1, dc in next dc) 3 times, (2 dc, ch 1, 2 dc) in next ch-2 sp, dc in next dc; repeat from ★ 2 times **more**, ch 1; join with slip st to third ch of beginning ch-4, finish off.

Rnd 4: With **right** side facing, join CC with sc in any corner ch-1 sp ***(see Joining With Sc, page 124)***; ch 2, sc in same sp, ★ sc in each st and in each ch-1 sp across to next corner ch-1 sp, (sc, ch 2, sc) in corner ch-1 sp; repeat from ★ 2 times **more**, sc in each st and in each ch-1 sp across; join with slip st to first sc: 52 sc.

Rnd 5: Slip st in first ch-2 sp, ch 1, 3 sc in same sp, skip next sc, sc in next 11 sc, skip next sc, ★ 3 sc in next ch-2 sp, skip next sc, sc in next 11 sc, skip next sc; repeat from ★ around; join with slip st to first sc, finish off: 56 sc.

Rnd 6: With **wrong** side facing, join MC with sc in same st as joining; ★ † (pull up a loop in same st and in next st, YO and draw through all 3 loops on hook) 12 times, ch 1, dc in next sc, ch 1 †, sc in next sc; repeat from ★ 2 times **more**, then repeat from † to † once; join with slip st to first sc, finish off.

Rnd 7: With **right** side facing, join CC with slip st in any corner dc; ch 3, (dc, ch 1, 2 dc) in same st, ★ † skip next ch, 2 dc in next st, (skip next st, 2 dc in next st) 6 times, skip next ch †, (2 dc, ch 1, 2 dc) in next corner dc; repeat from ★ 2 times **more**, then repeat from † to † once; join with slip st to top of beginning ch-3: 72 sts and 4 ch-1 sps.

Rnd 8: Slip st in next dc and in next ch-1 sp, ch 3, (dc, ch 1, 2 dc) in same sp, 2 dc in sp between each 2-dc group across to next corner ch-1 sp, ★ (2 dc, ch 1, 2 dc) in corner ch-1 sp, 2 dc in sp between each 2-dc group across to next corner ch-1 sp; repeat from ★ around; join with slip st to top of beginning ch-3, finish off: 80 sts.

ASSEMBLY

With CC, whipstitch Squares together ***(Fig. 32a, page 125)*** forming 4 vertical strips of 6 Squares each, beginning in first corner ch and ending in next corner ch; then whipstitch strips together in same manner.

DOUBLE PLAY

These playful designs and colorful creations offer fun in a flash! Using double strands of yarn and simple patterns means you can enjoy any one of these cheery throws in about half the time it usually takes to make an afghan. Youngsters — and the young at heart — will think the rainbow wraps are super! There's also a blanket of snuggly shell stitches in rich jewel tones, a coverlet with a flower patch of polka dots, and more.

CAREFREE FILET

Alternating rows of double crochet stitches and openwork create a lacy effect on this lovely filet throw. Worked up in ivory yarn sprinkled with bits of color, the speckled afghan is perfect for cool autumn weather.

Finished Size: Approximately 49" x 62"

MATERIALS

Worsted Weight Yarn, approximately:
49 ounces, (1,390 grams, 3,220 yards)
Crochet hook, size N (9.00 mm) **or** size needed for gauge

Note: Entire Afghan is worked holding two strands of yarn together.

GAUGE: 10 dc and 5 rows = 4"

Ch 119 **loosely**.

Row 1 (Right side)**:** Dc in fourth ch from hook **(3 skipped chs count as first dc)** and in each ch across: 117 dc.

Note: Loop a short piece of yarn around any stitch to mark last row as **right** side.

Row 2: Ch 4 **(counts as first dc plus ch 1, now and throughout)**, turn; skip next dc, dc in next dc, ★ ch 1, skip next dc, dc in next dc; repeat from ★ across: 58 ch-1 sps.

Row 3: Ch 3 **(counts as first dc, now and throughout)**, turn; dc in next ch-1 sp and in each dc and each ch-1 sp across: 117 dc.

Row 4: Ch 3, turn; dc in next 2 dc, ★ ch 1, skip next dc, dc in next 3 dc; repeat from ★ across to last 2 dc, ch 1, skip next dc, dc in last dc: 29 ch-1 sps.

Row 5: Ch 3, turn; dc in next ch-1 sp and in each dc and each ch-1 sp across: 117 dc.

Row 6: Ch 4, turn; skip next dc, dc in next 3 dc, ★ ch 1, skip next dc, dc in next 3 dc; repeat from ★ across: 29 ch-1 sps.

Row 7: Ch 3, turn; dc in next dc and in each dc and each ch-1 sp across: 117 dc.

Row 8: Ch 3, turn; dc in next 2 dc, ★ ch 1, skip next dc, dc in next 3 dc; repeat from ★ across to last 2 dc, ch 1, skip next dc, dc in last dc: 29 ch-1 sps.

Row 9: Ch 3, turn; dc in next ch-1 sp and in each dc and each ch-1 sp across: 117 dc.

Repeat Rows 2-9 until Afghan measures approximately 60" from beginning ch, ending by working Row 3; do **not** finish off.

EDGING

Rnd 1: Ch 1, do **not** turn; 3 sc in same st; work 149 sc evenly spaced across end of rows; working in free loops of beginning ch ***(Fig. 29b, page 124)***, 3 sc in first ch, sc in next 115 chs, 3 sc in next ch; work 149 sc evenly spaced across end of rows; 3 sc in next dc, sc in each dc across; join with slip st to first sc: 540 sc.

Rnd 2: Slip st in next sc, ch 4, (dc in same st, ch 1) twice, (skip next sc, dc in next sc, ch 1) across to within one sc of corner sc, ★ skip next sc, (dc, ch 1) 3 times in corner sc, (skip next sc, dc in next sc, ch 1) across to within one st of corner sc; repeat from ★ around; join with slip st to first dc.

Rnd 3: Ch 1, sc in same st and in each ch-1 sp and each dc around working 3 sc in each corner dc; join with slip st to first sc, finish off.

RAINBOW STRIPES

Rows of black boldly accentuate the colorful stripes of treble, half double, and single crochet stitches on our cheery throw. With its eye-catching waves, this afghan is sure be a child's favorite.

Finished Size: Approximately 43" x 57"

MATERIALS

Worsted Weight Yarn, approximately:

- MC (Black) - 10 ounces, (280 grams, 585 yards)
- Color A (Red) - $8^1/2$ ounces, (240 grams, 495 yards)
- Color B (Orange) - $8^1/2$ ounces, (240 grams, 495 yards)
- Color C (Yellow) - $8^1/2$ ounces, (240 grams, 495 yards)
- Color D (Green) - $8^1/2$ ounces, (240 grams, 495 yards)
- Color E (Blue) - $8^1/2$ ounces, (240 grams, 495 yards)
- Color F (Purple) - $8^1/2$ ounces, (240 grams, 495 yards)

Crochet hook, size N (9.00 mm) **or** size needed for gauge

Note: Entire Afghan is worked holding two strands of yarn together.

GAUGE: In pattern, 9 sts and 9 rows = 4"

STRIPE SEQUENCE

3 Rows MC ***(Fig. 30a, page 124)***, ★ 4 rows Color A, 2 rows MC, 4 rows Color B, 2 rows MC, 4 rows Color C, 2 rows MC, 4 rows Color D, 2 rows MC, 4 rows Color E, 2 rows MC, 4 rows Color F, 2 rows MC; repeat from ★ 2 times **more**, then work one **more** row MC.

With MC, ch 97 **loosely**.

Row 1 (Right side)**:** Sc in second ch from hook and in next ch, hdc in next 2 chs, dc in next 2 chs, tr in next 4 chs, dc in next 2 chs, hdc in next 2 chs, ★ sc in next 4 chs, hdc in next 2 chs, dc in next 2 chs, tr in next 4 chs, dc in next 2 chs, hdc in next 2 chs; repeat from ★ across to last 2 chs, sc in last 2 chs: 96 sts.

Note: Loop a short piece of yarn around any stitch to mark last row as **right** side.

Rows 2-4: Ch 1, turn; sc in each st across.

Rows 5 and 6: Ch 4, turn; tr in next st, dc in next 2 sts, hdc in next 2 sts, sc in next 4 sts, hdc in next 2 sts, dc in next 2 sts, ★ tr in next 4 sts, dc in next 2 sts, hdc in next 2 sts, sc in next 4 sts, hdc in next 2 sts, dc in next 2 sts; repeat from ★ across to last 2 sts, tr in last 2 sts.

Rows 7-10: Ch 1, turn; sc in each st across.

Rows 11 and 12: Ch 1, turn; sc in first 2 sts, hdc in next 2 sts, dc in next 2 sts, tr in next 4 sts, dc in next 2 sts, hdc in next 2 sts, ★ sc in next 4 sts, hdc in next 2 sts, dc in next 2 sts, tr in next 4 sts, dc in next 2 sts, hdc in next 2 sts; repeat from ★ across to last 2 sts, sc in last 2 sts.

Rows 13-16: Ch 1, turn; sc in each st across.

Rows 17-111: Repeat Rows 5-16, 7 times; then repeat Rows 5-15 once **more**.

Row 112: Ch 4, turn; tr in next sc, dc in next 2 sc, hdc in next 2 sc, sc in next 4 sc, hdc in next 2 sc, dc in next 2 sc, ★ tr in next 4 sc, dc in next 2 sc, hdc in next 2 sc, sc in next 4 sc, hdc in next 2 sc, dc in next 2 sc; repeat from ★ across to last 2 sc, tr in last 2 sc; finish off.

EDGING

With **right** side facing, join MC with slip st in any st; ch 1, sc evenly around working 3 sc in each corner; join with slip st to first sc, finish off.

NAUTILUS

Featuring a luxurious blanket of lavender V-stitches and shells, this afghan will remind you of idyllic days spent at the beach. You'll welcome its warming comfort as the day fades into cool evening.

Finished Size: Approximately 45" x 60"

MATERIALS

Worsted Weight Yarn, approximately:
46 ounces, (1,310 grams, 3,140 yards)
Crochet hook, size P (10.00 mm) **or** size needed for gauge

Note: Entire Afghan is worked holding two strands of yarn together.

GAUGE: (Shell, V-St) and 4 rows = $3^{1}/_{2}$"

PATTERN STITCHES

V-ST

(Dc, ch 1, dc) in st or sp indicated.

SHELL

7 Dc in st indicated.

Ch 127 **loosely**.

Row 1 (Right side)**:** Work V-St in fifth ch from hook, ★ skip next 4 chs, work Shell in next ch, skip next 4 chs, work V-St in next ch; repeat from ★ across to last 2 chs, skip next ch, dc in last ch: 13 V-Sts.

Note: Loop a short piece of yarn around any stitch to mark last row as **right** side.

Row 2: Ch 3 **(counts as first dc, now and throughout)**, turn; work V-St in next ch-1 sp, ★ ch 3, skip next 4 dc, sc in next dc, ch 3, work V-St in next ch-1 sp; repeat from ★ across to last 2 sts, skip next dc, dc in top of beginning ch.

Row 3: Ch 3, turn; work V-St in next ch-1 sp, ★ work Shell in next sc, work V-St in next ch-1 sp; repeat from ★ across to last 2 dc, skip next dc, dc in last dc.

Row 4: Ch 3, turn; work V-St in next ch-1 sp, ★ ch 3, skip next 4 dc, sc in next dc, ch 3, work V-St in next ch-1 sp; repeat from ★ across to last 2 dc, skip next dc, dc in last dc.

Repeat Rows 3 and 4 until Afghan measures approximately 58" from beginning ch, ending by working Row 4; do **not** finish off.

EDGING

Rnd 1: Ch 1, turn; (sc, ch 1, sc) in first dc, work 99 sc evenly spaced across to last dc, (sc, ch 1, sc) in last dc; work 131 sc evenly spaced across end of rows; working in free loops of beginning ch ***(Fig. 29b, page 124)***, (sc, ch 1, sc) in first ch, work 99 sc evenly spaced across to corner ch, (sc, ch 1, sc) in corner ch; work 131 sc evenly spaced across end of rows; join with slip st to first sc: 468 sc.

Rnd 2: Slip st in first ch-1 sp, ch 1, (sc in same sp, ch 2) twice, ★ † skip next sc, (sc in next sc, ch 2, skip next sc) across to next ch-1 sp †, (sc, ch 2) twice in ch-1 sp; repeat from ★ 2 times **more**, then repeat from † to † once; join with slip st to first sc, finish off.

TRUE BLUE RIPPLES

A true blue buddy for an old-fashioned hayride, this comfy wrap is worked in gently rolling ripples. The lacy pattern is created using treble and half double crochet stitches.

Finished Size: Approximately 48" x 61"

MATERIALS

Worsted Weight Yarn, approximately:
41 ounces, (1,160 grams, 3,045 yards)
Crochet hook, size N (9.00 mm) **or** size needed for gauge

Note: Entire Afghan is worked holding two strands of yarn together.

GAUGE: One repeat (19 sts) = 8"

Ch 117 **loosely**.

Row 1 (Right side)**:** Hdc in third ch from hook **(2 skipped chs count as first hdc)** and in each ch across: 116 hdc.

Note #1: Loop a short piece of yarn around any stitch to mark last row as **right** side.

Note #2: To work **hdc decrease** (uses next 3 hdc), YO, insert hook in next hdc, YO and pull up a loop, YO, skip next hdc, insert hook in next hdc, YO and pull up a loop, YO and draw through all 5 loops on hook ***(Fig. 22, page 122)*** **(counts as one hdc)**.

Row 2: Ch 2 **(counts as first hdc, now and throughout)**, turn; hdc in next 8 hdc, hdc decrease, ★ hdc in next 7 hdc, 2 hdc in each of next 2 hdc, hdc in next 7 hdc, hdc decrease; repeat from ★ across to last 9 hdc, hdc in last 9 hdc: 114 hdc.

Row 3: Ch 2, turn; hdc in next hdc and in each hdc across.

Note: To work **tr decrease** (uses next 3 hdc), YO twice, insert hook in next hdc, YO and pull up a loop, (YO and draw through 2 loops on hook) twice, YO twice, skip next hdc, insert hook in next hdc, YO and pull up a loop, (YO and draw through 2 loops on hook) twice, YO and draw through all 3 loops on hook ***(Fig. 24, page 122)*** **(counts as one tr)**.

Row 4: Ch 5 **(counts as first tr plus ch 1)**, turn; (tr in same st, ch 1) twice, ★ † (skip next hdc, tr in next hdc) 3 times, skip next hdc, tr decrease, (skip next hdc, tr in next hdc) 3 times, ch 1, skip next hdc, tr in next hdc, (ch 1, tr in same st) twice †, (tr, ch 1) 3 times in next hdc; repeat from ★ 4 times **more**, then repeat from † to † once: 78 tr.

Row 5: Ch 2, turn; hdc in first tr and in each ch and each tr across to last tr, 2 hdc in last tr: 116 hdc.

Repeat Rows 2-5 until Afghan measures approximately 61" from beginning ch, ending by working Row 3.

Finish off.

RAINBOW GRANNY

Brilliantly colored medallions are simply whipstitched together to form this attention-getting afghan. Worked in extra-easy granny squares, it's a great choice for beginners!

Finished Size: Approximately 50" x 63"

MATERIALS

Worsted Weight Yarn, approximately:
- MC (Black) - 25½ ounces, (720 grams, 1,490 yards)
- Color A (Red) - 8½ ounces, (240 grams, 495 yards)
- Color B (Orange) - 10½ ounces, (300 grams, 615 yards)
- Color C (Yellow) - 6½ ounces, (180 grams, 380 yards)
- Color D (Green) - 6½ ounces, (180 grams, 380 yards)
- Color E (Blue) - 10½ ounces, (300 grams, 615 yards)
- Color F (Purple) - 8½ ounces, (240 grams, 495 yards)

Crochet hook, size N (9.00 mm) **or** size needed for gauge
Yarn needle

Note: Entire Afghan is worked holding two strands of yarn together.

GAUGE: Each Square = 12½"

SQUARE

Make 10 **each** in the following color sequences:

	Square #1	Square #2
Rnd 1	Color A	Color F
Rnd 2	Color B	Color E
Rnd 3	Color C	Color D
Rnd 4	Color D	Color C
Rnd 5	Color E	Color B
Rnd 6	Color E	Color B
Rnd 7	Color F	Color A
Rnd 8	MC	MC
Rnd 9	MC	MC

With first color, ch 6; join with slip st to form a ring.

Rnd 1 (Right side)**:** Ch 3 **(counts as first dc, now and throughout)**, 15 dc in ring; join with slip st to first dc, finish off: 16 dc.

Note: Loop a short piece of yarn around any stitch to mark last round as **right** side.

Rnd 2: With **right** side facing, join next color with slip st in any dc; ch 3, 2 dc in same st, ch 1, skip next dc, ★ 3 dc in next dc, ch 1, skip next dc; repeat from ★ around; join with slip st to first dc, finish off: 24 dc.

Rnd 3: With **right** side facing, join next color with slip st in any ch-1 sp; ch 3, dc in same sp, ch 1, skip next dc, 2 dc in next dc, ch 1, ★ 2 dc in next ch-1 sp, ch 1, skip next dc, 2 dc in next dc, ch 1; repeat from ★ around; join with slip st to first dc, finish off: 16 ch-1 sps.

Rnd 4: With **right** side facing, join next color with slip st in any ch-1 sp; ch 1, sc in same sp, ch 4, (sc in next ch-1 sp, ch 4) around; join with slip st to first sc, finish off.

Rnd 5: With **right** side facing, join next color with slip st in any ch-4 sp; ch 1, sc in same sp, ch 4, (sc in next ch-4 sp, ch 4) around; join with slip st to first sc.

Rnd 6: Slip st in first ch-4 sp, ch 3, 3 dc in same sp, 4 dc in each ch-4 sp around; join with slip st to first dc, finish off: 64 dc.

Rnd 7: With **right** side facing, join next color with slip st in sp **before** third dc of any 4-dc group; ch 3, dc in same sp, ch 1, skip next 2 dc, ★ 2 dc in sp **before** next dc, ch 1, skip next 2 dc; repeat from ★ around; join with slip st to first dc, finish off: 32 ch-1 sps.

Rnd 8: With **right** side facing, join MC with slip st in any ch-1 sp; ch 3, (dc, ch 2, 2 dc) in same sp, dc in next 2 dc, (skip next ch-1 sp, dc in next 2 dc) 7 times, ★ (2 dc, ch 2, 2 dc) in next ch-1 sp, dc in next 2 dc, (skip next ch-1 sp, dc in next 2 dc) 7 times; repeat from ★ around; join with slip st to first dc: 80 dc.

Rnd 9: Ch 3, dc in next dc, (3 dc, ch 2, 3 dc) in next ch-2 sp, ★ dc in each dc across to next ch-2 sp, (3 dc, ch 2, 3 dc) in ch-2 sp; repeat from ★ 2 times **more**, dc in each dc across; join with slip st to first dc, finish off.

ASSEMBLY

With MC, whipstitch Squares together as follows ***(Fig. 32b, page 125)***, beginning in second ch of first corner ch-2 sp and ending in first ch of next corner ch-2 sp:

Alternating Square #1 and Square #2, form 2 vertical strips with Square #1 as first and last Square and form 2 vertical strips with Square #2 as first and last Square.

Join strips in same manner.

EDGING

With **right** side facing, join MC with slip st in any st; ch 1, sc evenly around working 3 sc in each corner; join with slip st to first sc, finish off.

POLKA DOT PATCH

Sprinkled with polka dots, this pretty afghan is perfect to take along on a springtime picnic. There's an easy-to-follow placement chart that shows you how to join the motifs as you go.

Finished Size: Approximately 47" x 67"

MATERIALS

Worsted Weight Yarn, approximately:
MC (White) - 37 ounces, (1,050 grams, 2,535 yards)
Colors A thru F (Pink, Peach, Yellow, Mint, Blue, and Lavender) - 3 ounces, (90 grams, 205 yards) **each**
Crochet hook, size P (10.00 mm) **or** size needed for gauge

Note: Entire Afghan is worked holding two strands of yarn together.

GAUGE: Each Motif = 6½" (point to point)

Note: Following Placement Chart, make Motifs using color indicated.

FIRST MOTIF

Ch 6; join with slip st to form a ring.
Rnd 1 (Right side)**:** Ch 3, 2 dc in ring, ch 2, (3 dc in ring, ch 2) 5 times; join with slip st to top of beginning ch-3, finish off: 6 ch-2 sps.
Note: Loop a short piece of yarn around any stitch to mark last round as **right** side.
Rnd 2: With **right** side facing, join MC with slip st in any ch-2 sp; ch 3, (2 dc, ch 2, 3 dc) in same sp, ch 1, ★ (3 dc, ch 2, 3 dc) in next ch-2 sp, ch 1; repeat from ★ around; join with slip st to top of beginning ch-3, finish off: 12 sps.

ADDITIONAL MOTIFS

Ch 6; join with slip st to form a ring.
Rnd 1 (Right side)**:** Ch 3, 2 dc in ring, ch 2, (3 dc in ring, ch 2) 5 times; join with slip st to top of beginning ch-3, finish off: 6 ch-2 sps.
Note: Mark last round as **right** side.
Rnd 2: Work One, Two, or Three Side Joining ***(Fig. 21, page 122)***.

ONE SIDE JOINING

Rnd 2: With **right** side facing, join MC with slip st in any ch-2 sp; ch 3, 2 dc in same sp, ch 1, ★ (3 dc, ch 2, 3 dc) in next ch-2 sp, ch 1; repeat from ★ 3 times **more**, 3 dc in next ch-2 sp, ch 1, holding Motifs with **wrong** sides together, slip st in ch-2 sp on **previous Motif**, ch 1, 3 dc in same sp on **new Motif**, ch 1, slip st in next ch-1 sp on **previous Motif**, 3 dc in same sp as beginning ch-3 on **new Motif**, ch 1, slip st in next ch-2 sp on **previous Motif**, ch 1; join with slip st to top of beginning ch-3, finish off.

TWO SIDE JOINING

Rnd 2: With **right** side facing, join MC with slip st in any ch-2 sp; ch 3, 2 dc in same sp, ch 1, ★ (3 dc, ch 2, 3 dc) in next ch-2 sp, ch 1; repeat from ★ 2 times **more**, 3 dc in next ch-2 sp, ch 1, holding Motifs with **wrong** sides together, † slip st in ch-2 sp on **previous Motif**, ch 1, 3 dc in same sp on **new Motif**, ch 1, slip st in next ch-1 sp on **previous Motif** †, 3 dc in next ch-2 sp on **new Motif**, ch 1, slip st in next ch-2 sp on **previous Motif**, ch 1, repeat from † to † once, 3 dc in same ch-2 sp as beginning ch-3 on **new Motif**, ch 1, slip st in next ch-2 sp on **previous Motif**, ch 1; join with slip st to top of beginning ch-3, finish off.

PLACEMENT CHART

THREE SIDE JOINING

Rnd 2: With **right** side facing, join MC with slip st in any ch-2 sp; ch 3, 2 dc in same sp, ch 1, ★ (3 dc, ch 2, 3 dc) in next ch-2 sp, ch 1; repeat from ★ once **more**, 3 dc in next ch-2 sp, ch 1, holding Motifs with **wrong** sides together, slip st in ch-2 sp on **previous Motif**, ch 1, 3 dc in same sp on **new Motif**, ch 1, slip st in next ch-1 sp on **previous Motif**, † 3 dc in next ch-2 sp on **new Motif**, ch 1, (slip st in ch-2 sp on **previous Motif**, ch 1) twice, 3 dc in same sp on **new Motif**, ch 1, slip st in next ch-1 sp on **previous Motif** †, repeat from † to † once **more**, 3 dc in same ch-2 sp as beginning ch-3 on **new Motif**, ch 1, slip st in next ch-2 sp on **previous Motif**, ch 1; join with slip st to top of beginning ch-3, finish off.

EDGING

Note: To work **decrease**, insert hook in next ch, YO and pull up a loop, skip joining, insert hook in next ch, YO and pull up a loop, YO and draw through all 3 loops on hook.

With **right** side facing, join MC with slip st in first ch of any ch-2 sp; ch 1, sc in each ch and in each dc around decreasing at each joining; join with slip st to first sc, finish off.

SEA PEACH

Beachcombers and landlubbers alike will love this peachy afghan! Featuring soft bubble shells that resemble sand dollars, it has a scalloped edging.

Finished Size: Approximately 47" x 62"

MATERIALS

Worsted Weight Yarn, approximately:
75 ounces, (2,130 grams, 5,145 yards)
Crochet hook, size P (10.00 mm) **or** size needed for gauge

Note: Entire Afghan is worked holding two strands of yarn together.

GAUGE: One Shell = 3" and 3 rows = 3 1/4"

Note: To work **Shell**, (4 tr, ch 1, 4 tr) in st indicated.

Ch 122 **loosely**.

Row 1: Sc in second ch from hook, skip next 3 chs, work Shell in next ch, ★ skip next 3 chs, slip st in next ch, skip next 3 chs, work Shell in next ch; repeat from ★ across to last 4 chs, skip next 3 chs, sc in last ch: 15 Shells.

Row 2 (Right side)**:** Ch 4 **(counts as first tr, now and throughout)**, turn; working in Back Loops Only ***(Fig. 28, page 124)***, 3 tr in same st, skip next 4 tr, slip st in next ch, ★ skip next 4 tr, work Shell in next slip st, skip next 4 tr, slip st in next ch; repeat from ★ across to last 5 sts, skip next 4 tr, 4 tr in last sc: 14 Shells.

Note: Loop a short piece of yarn around any stitch to mark last row as **right** side.

Row 3: Ch 1, turn; working in Back Loops Only, sc in first tr, skip next 3 tr, work Shell in next slip st, ★ skip next 4 tr, slip st in next ch, skip next 4 tr, work Shell in next slip st; repeat from ★ across to last 4 tr, skip next 3 tr, sc in last tr: 15 Shells.

Row 4: Ch 4, turn; working in Back Loops Only, 3 tr in same st, skip next 4 tr, slip st in next ch, ★ skip next 4 tr, work Shell in next slip st, skip next 4 tr, slip st in next ch; repeat from ★ across to last 5 sts, skip next 4 tr, 4 tr in last sc: 14 Shells.

Repeat Rows 3 and 4 until Afghan measures approximately 59" from beginning ch, ending by working Row 4.

Last Row: Ch 1, turn; working in Back Loops Only, sc in first tr, ch 3, skip next 3 tr, tr in next slip st, ch 3, ★ skip next 4 tr, sc in next ch, ch 3, skip next 4 tr, tr in next slip st, ch 3; repeat from ★ across to last 4 tr, skip next 3 tr, sc in last tr; do **not** finish off: 30 ch-3 sps.

EDGING

Rnd 1: Ch 1, turn; working in both loops, (sc, ch 1, sc) in first sc, work 104 sc evenly spaced across to last sc, (sc, ch 1, sc) in last sc; work 134 sc evenly spaced across end of rows; working in free loops of beginning ch ***(Fig. 29b, page 124)***, (sc, ch 1, sc) in ch at base of first sc, work 104 sc evenly spaced across to last ch, (sc, ch 1, sc) in last ch; work 134 sc evenly spaced across end of rows; join with slip st to first sc: 484 sc.

Rnd 2: Slip st in next ch-1 sp and in next sc, ch 1, (sc, ch 2, dc, ch 2, sc) in same st, ★ † [skip next 2 sc, (sc, ch 2, dc, ch 2, sc) in next sc] across to next ch-1 sp, skip ch-1 sp †, (sc, ch 2, dc, ch 2, sc) in next sc; repeat from ★ 2 times **more**, then repeat from † to † once; join with slip st to first sc, finish off.

BLENDED RAINBOW

Quick to crochet using basic stitches and working lengthwise, this vibrant afghan brings the magic of a rainbow into your child's room! The blended effect is created by holding strands of two different colors together while stitching between the solid colored stripes. A flowing fringe finishes this just-for-fun throw.

Finished Size: Approximately 44" x 60"

MATERIALS

Worsted Weight Yarn, approximately:
- Color A (Red) - 10 ounces, (280 grams, 585 yards)
- Color B (Orange) - 13 ounces, (370 grams, 760 yards)
- Color C (Yellow) - 13 ounces, (370 grams, 760 yards)
- Color D (Green) - 13 ounces, (370 grams, 760 yards)
- Color E (Blue) - 13 ounces, (370 grams, 760 yards)
- Color F (Purple) - 10 ounces, (280 grams, 585 yards)

Crochet hook, size N (9.00 mm) **or** size needed for gauge

Note: Each row is worked across length of Afghan holding two strands of yarn together. When joining yarn and finishing off, leave an 8" length at end to be worked into fringe.

GAUGE: In pattern, five 2-dc groups = $4^1/_2$"
and 6 rows = 4"

Holding two strands of Color A together, ch 124 **loosely**.

Row 1 (Right side)**:** Dc in fourth ch from hook, (skip next ch, 2 dc in next ch) across: 122 sts.

Note: Loop a short piece of yarn around any stitch to mark last row as **right** side.

Row 2: Ch 3 **(counts as first dc, now and throughout)**, turn; skip next dc, 2 dc in sp **before** next dc, (skip next 2 dc, 2 dc in sp **before** next dc) across to last 2 sts, skip next dc, dc in top of beginning ch.

Row 3: Ch 3, turn; dc in sp **before** next dc, (skip next 2 dc, 2 dc in sp **before** next dc) across.

Row 4: Ch 3, turn; skip next dc, 2 dc in sp **before** next dc, (skip next 2 dc, 2 dc in sp **before** next dc) across to last 2 dc, skip next dc, dc in last dc.

Rows 5 and 6: Repeat Rows 3 and 4.

Finish off.

Row 7: Holding one strand of Color A and one strand of Color B together and with **right** side facing, join yarn with slip st in first dc; ch 3, dc in sp **before** next dc, (skip next 2 dc, 2 dc in sp **before** next dc) across.

Row 8: Ch 3, turn; skip next dc, 2 dc in sp **before** next dc, (skip next 2 dc, 2 dc in sp **before** next dc) across to last 2 dc, skip next dc, dc in last dc.

Row 9: Ch 3, turn; dc in sp **before** next dc, (skip next 2 dc, 2 dc in sp **before** next dc) across.

Row 10: Ch 3, turn; skip next dc, 2 dc in sp **before** next dc, (skip next 2 dc, 2 dc in sp **before** next dc) across to last 2 dc, skip next dc, dc in last dc.

Rows 11 and 12: Repeat Rows 9 and 10.

Finish off.

Rows 13-18: Holding two strands of Color B together, repeat Rows 7-12; at end of Row 18, finish off.

Rows 19-24: Holding one strand of Color B and one strand of Color C together, repeat Rows 7-12; at end of Row 24, finish off.

Rows 25-30: Holding two strands of Color C together, repeat Rows 7-12; at end of Row 30, finish off.

Rows 31-36: Holding one strand of Color C and one strand of Color D together, repeat Rows 7-12; at end of Row 36, finish off.

Rows 37-42: Holding two strands of Color D together, repeat Rows 7-12; at end of Row 42, finish off.
Rows 43-48: Holding one strand of Color D and one strand of Color E together, repeat Rows 7-12; at end of Row 48, finish off.
Rows 49-54: Holding two strands of Color E together, repeat Rows 7-12; at end of Row 54, finish off.
Rows 55-60: Holding one strand of Color E and one strand of Color F together, repeat Rows 7-12; at end of Row 60, finish off.
Rows 61-66: Holding two strands of Color F together, repeat Rows 7-12; at end of Row 66, finish off.

On fringed end of Afghan, add additional fringe ***(Figs. 33b & d, page 126)*** using three 17" strands of corresponding colors. On opposite end of Afghan, add fringe using four 17" strands of corresponding colors.

SOUTHWESTERN STRIPES

This handsome striped afghan will add a touch of the Southwest to your home. Diamond clusters and simple post stitches give the cozy wrap added texture, so it's great for snuggling up in, too.

Finished Size: Approximately 48" x 63"

MATERIALS

Worsted Weight Yarn, approximately:
MC (Cream) - 60 ounces, (1,700 grams, 3,500 yards)
Color A (Blue) - 7 ounces, (200 grams, 410 yards)
Color B (Peach) - 7 ounces, (200 grams, 410 yards)
Color C (Green) - 7 ounces, (200 grams, 410 yards)
Crochet hook, size N (9.00 mm) **or** size needed for gauge

Note: Each row is worked across length of Afghan holding two strands of yarn together.

GAUGE: In pattern, 9 sts and 8 rows = 4"

PATTERN STITCHES

FRONT POST DOUBLE CROCHET ***(abbreviated FPdc)***

YO, insert hook from **front** to **back** around post of st indicated, YO and pull up a loop even with last st made (3 loops on hook) ***(Fig. 10, page 119)***, (YO and draw through 2 loops on hook) twice. Skip sc behind FPdc.

CLUSTER

★ YO, insert hook from **front** to **back** around post of dc indicated, YO and pull up a loop even with last st made, YO and draw through 2 loops on hook; repeat from ★ once **more**, YO and draw through all 3 loops on hook ***(Figs. 16a & b, page 120)***. Skip sc behind Cluster.

With MC, ch 138 **loosely**.

Row 1: Sc in second ch from hook and in each ch across: 137 sc.

Row 2 (Right side)**:** Ch 3 **(counts as first dc, now and throughout)**, turn; dc in next sc and in each sc across.

Note: Loop a short piece of yarn around any stitch to mark last row as **right** side.

Row 3: Ch 1, turn; sc in each dc across.

Row 4: Ch 3, turn; dc in next sc, (work FPdc around dc in row **below** next sc, dc in next 2 sc) across: 45 FPdc.

Row 5: Ch 1, turn; sc in each st across changing to Color A in last sc ***(Fig. 30a, page 124)***.

Row 6: Ch 3, turn; dc in next sc, (work FPdc around FPdc in row **below** next sc, dc in next 2 sc) across: 45 FPdc.

Row 7: Ch 1, turn; sc in each st across changing to MC in last sc.

Rows 8-17: Repeat Rows 6 and 7, 5 times, working in the following color sequence: 2 Rows **each** MC, Color B, MC, Color C, MC; at end of Row 17, do **not** change colors.

Row 18: Ch 3, turn; dc in next sc and in each sc across.

Row 19: Ch 1, turn; sc in each st across.

Row 20: Ch 3, turn; dc in next 7 sc, work Cluster around dc in row **below** next sc, (dc in next 5 sc, work Cluster around dc in row **below** next sc) across to last 8 sc, dc in last 8 sc: 21 Clusters.

Row 21: Ch 1, turn; sc in each st across.

Row 22: Ch 3, turn; dc in next 6 sc, work Cluster around dc in row **below** next sc, dc in next sc, work Cluster around dc in row **below** next sc, ★ dc in next 3 sc, work Cluster around dc in row **below** next sc, dc in next sc, work Cluster around dc in row **below** next sc; repeat from ★ across to last 7 sc, dc in last 7 sc: 42 Clusters.

Rows 23-25: Repeat Rows 19-21.

Row 26: Ch 3, turn; dc in next sc and in each sc across.

Rows 27-91: Repeat Rows 3-26 twice, then repeat Rows 3-19 once **more**; do **not** finish off.

EDGING

Rnd 1: Ch 3, turn; (dc, ch 1, 2 dc) in first sc, (skip next sc, 2 dc in next sc) across to last 2 sc, skip next sc, (2 dc, ch 1, 2 dc) in last sc; skip first sc row, (2 dc in end of next dc row, skip next sc row) across; working in free loops of beginning ch ***(Fig. 29b, page 124)***, (2 dc, ch 1, 2 dc) in ch at base of first sc, (skip next ch, 2 dc in next ch) across to last 2 chs, skip next ch, (2 dc, ch 1, 2 dc) in last ch; skip first sc row, (2 dc in end of next dc row, skip next sc row) across; join with slip st to first dc: 464 dc.

Rnd 2: Ch 1, turn; sc in each dc around working 3 sc in each corner ch-1 sp; join with slip st to first sc, finish off.

CAPTIVATING SHELLS

Rich textures and soft jewel-tone yarns lend a captivating air to this dreamy afghan. Back post and front post double crochet stitches form the ridges that separate the lavish shells.

Finished Size: Approximately 51" x 68"

MATERIALS

Worsted Weight Yarn, approximately:
MC (Teal) - 60 ounces, (1,700 grams, 2,740 yards)
CC (Variegated) - 14 ounces, (400 grams, 640 yards)
Crochet hook, size N (9.00 mm) **or** size needed for gauge

Note: Entire Afghan is worked holding two strands of yarn together.

GAUGE: 10 dc and 6 rows = 4"

PATTERN STITCHES

BACK POST DOUBLE CROCHET ***(abbreviated BPdc)***
YO, insert hook from **back** to **front** around post of st indicated, YO and pull up a loop even with last st made (3 loops on hook) ***(Fig. 12, page 119)***, (YO and draw through 2 loops on hook) twice.

FRONT POST DOUBLE CROCHET ***(abbreviated FPdc)***
YO, insert hook from **front** to **back** around post of st indicated, YO and pull up a loop even with last st made (3 loops on hook) ***(Fig. 10, page 119)***, (YO and draw through 2 loops on hook) twice.

STRIPE SEQUENCE

2 Rows of one strand MC and one strand CC ***(Fig. 30a, page 124)***, ★ 1 row of two strands MC, 2 rows of one strand MC and one strand CC; repeat from ★ throughout.

Holding one strand of MC and one strand of CC together, ch 126 **loosely**.

Row 1 (Right side)**:** Dc in sixth ch from hook, ★ skip next 2 chs, 5 dc in next ch, skip next 2 chs, dc in next ch, ch 1, skip next ch, dc in next ch; repeat from ★ across: 16 sps.

Note: Loop a short piece of yarn around any stitch to mark last row as **right** side.

Row 2: Ch 4 **(counts as first dc plus ch 1, now and throughout)**, turn; work BPdc around next dc, skip next 2 dc, 5 dc in next dc, skip next 2 dc, work BPdc around next dc, ★ ch 1, work BPdc around next dc, skip next 2 dc, 5 dc in next dc, skip next 2 dc, work BPdc around next dc; repeat from ★ across to last sp, ch 1, skip next ch, dc in next ch.

Row 3: Ch 4, turn; work FPdc around next BPdc, skip next 2 dc, 5 dc in next dc, skip next 2 dc, work FPdc around next BPdc, ★ ch 1, work FPdc around next BPdc, skip next 2 dc, 5 dc in next dc, skip next 2 dc, work FPdc around next BPdc; repeat from ★ across to last dc, ch 1, dc in last dc.

Row 4: Ch 4, turn; work BPdc around next FPdc, skip next 2 dc, 5 dc in next dc, skip next 2 dc, work BPdc around next FPdc, ★ ch 1, work BPdc around next FPdc, skip next 2 dc, 5 dc in next dc, skip next 2 dc, work BPdc around next FPdc; repeat from ★ across to last dc, ch 1, dc in last dc.

Repeat Rows 3 and 4 until Afghan measures approximately 68" from beginning ch, ending by working 2 rows of one strand MC and one strand CC.

Finish off.

DOUBLY DELIGHTFUL

Worked in soothing hues and delicate patterns, our dreamy wraps are perfect for pampering yourself or that special someone! Feminine scallops, fanciful shells, and lacy V-stitches lend a genteel air to these lovelies. They make delightful additions to the bedroom or any place you want to add a soft touch. The downy baby afghans offer a lap of luxury for little ones, and you'll feel like you're in heaven when you curl up with one of the full-size throws!

GRACEFUL TRELLIS

Double crochet and versatile V-stitches create a latticework trellis on this light and airy summer afghan. Flowing fringe gives our throw a feminine finish.

Finished Size: Approximately 48" x 70"

MATERIALS

Worsted Weight Yarn, approximately:
75 ounces, (2,130 grams, 4,375 yards)
Crochet hook, size P (10.00 mm) **or** size needed for gauge

Note: Entire Afghan is worked holding two strands of yarn together.

GAUGE: 10 dc and 5 rows = 4"

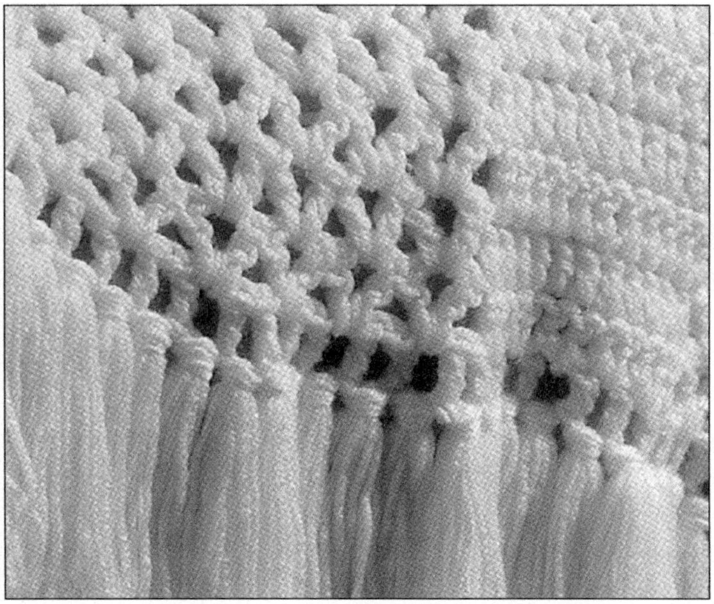

Ch 138 **loosely**.

Row 1 (Right side)**:** Dc in sixth ch from hook, ★ ch 1, skip next ch, dc in next ch; repeat from ★ across: 67 sps.

Note #1: Loop a short piece of yarn around any stitch to mark last row as **right** side.

Note #2: To work **V-St**, (dc, ch 2, dc) in sp indicated.

Row 2: Ch 4 **(counts as first dc plus ch 1, now and throughout)**, turn; (skip next ch-1 sp, work V-St in next ch-1 sp) 6 times, ch 1, ★ skip next ch-1 sp, dc in next dc, (dc in next ch-1 sp, dc in next dc) 5 times, ch 1, (skip next ch-1 sp, work V-St in next ch-1 sp) 6 times, ch 1; repeat from ★ 2 times **more**, skip next dc and next ch, dc in next ch: 24 V-Sts.

Row 3: Ch 4, turn; work V-St in next 6 V-Sts (ch-2 sp), ch 1, ★ skip next dc, dc in next 11 dc, ch 1, work V-St in next 6 V-Sts, ch 1; repeat from ★ across to last 2 dc, skip next dc, dc in last dc.

Repeat Row 3 until Afghan measures approximately 69" from beginning ch, ending by working a **wrong** side row.

Last Row: Ch 4, turn; dc in next dc, (ch 1, dc in next dc) 12 times, ★ (ch 1, skip next dc, dc in next dc) 5 times, (ch 1, dc in next dc) 13 times; repeat from ★ across; finish off: 67 ch-1 sps.

Using ten 17" strands, add fringe across short edges of Afghan ***(Figs. 33a & c, page 126)***.

CHARMING WRAP

The charming windowpane pattern on this soft wrap reflects the colors of a fresh spring day. Worked in rounds, the pretty throw features a picot edging.

Finished Size: Approximately 52¹/2" x 52¹/2"

MATERIALS

Worsted Weight Brushed Acrylic Yarn, approximately:
MC (Yellow) - 29¹/2 ounces, (840 grams, 2,275 yards)
CC (Blue) - 15¹/2 ounces, (440 grams, 1,195 yards)
Crochet hook, size N (9.00 mm) **or** size needed for gauge

Note: Entire Afghan is worked holding two strands of yarn together.

GAUGE: Rnds 1-7 = 10"

With MC, ch 5; join with slip st to form a ring.

Rnd 1 (Right side)**:** Ch 3 **(counts as first dc, now and throughout)**, 2 dc in ring, ch 1, (3 dc in ring, ch 1) 3 times; join with slip st to first dc, finish off: 12 dc.

Note: Loop a short piece of yarn around any stitch to mark last round as **right** side.

Rnd 2: With **right** side facing, join CC with sc in any ch-1 sp ***(see Joining With Sc, page 124)***; ch 3, sc in same sp, ch 3, (sc, ch 3) twice in each ch-1 sp around; join with slip st to first sc, finish off: 8 ch-3 sps.

Rnd 3: With **right** side facing, join MC with slip st in any corner ch-3 sp; ch 3, (2 dc, ch 1, 3 dc) in same sp, ch 1, 3 dc in next ch-3 sp, ch 1, ★ (3 dc, ch 1) twice in next ch-3 sp, 3 dc in next ch-3 sp, ch 1; repeat from ★ around; join with slip st to first dc, finish off: 36 dc.

Rnd 4: With **right** side facing, join CC with sc in any corner ch-1 sp; ch 3, sc in same sp, ch 3, (sc in next ch-1 sp, ch 3) across to next corner ch-1 sp, ★ (sc, ch 3) twice in corner ch-1 sp, (sc in next ch-1 sp, ch 3) across to next corner ch-1 sp; repeat from ★ around; join with slip st to first sc, finish off: 16 ch-3 sps.

Rnd 5: With **right** side facing, join MC with slip st in any corner ch-3 sp; ch 3, (2 dc, ch 1, 3 dc) in same sp, ch 1, (3 dc in next ch-3 sp, ch 1) across to next corner ch-3 sp, ★ (3 dc, ch 1) twice in corner ch-3 sp, (3 dc in next ch-3 sp, ch 1) across to next corner ch-3 sp; repeat from ★ around; join with slip st to first dc, finish off: 60 dc.

Rnds 6-34: Repeat Rnds 4 and 5, 14 times; then repeat Rnd 4 once **more**; at end of Rnd 34, do **not** finish off: 136 ch-3 sps.

Rnds 35 and 36: Slip st in first ch-3 sp, ch 1, (sc in same sp, ch 3) twice, (sc in next ch-3 sp, ch 3) across to next corner ch-3 sp, ★ (sc, ch 3) twice in corner ch-3 sp, (sc in next ch-3 sp, ch 3) across to next corner ch-3 sp; repeat from ★ around; join with slip st to first sc: 144 ch-3 sps.

Note: To work **Picot**, ch 3, slip st in third ch from hook.

Rnd 37: Slip st in first ch-3 sp, ch 3, work (2 dc, Picot, 3 dc, Picot) in same sp, (3 dc in next ch-3 sp, work Picot) across to next corner ch-3 sp, ★ (3 dc, work Picot) twice in corner ch-3 sp, (3 dc in next ch-3 sp, work Picot) across to next corner ch-3 sp; repeat from ★ around; join with slip st to first dc, finish off.

BABY-SOFT RAINBOW

This afghan for baby is a rainbow of pastel colors. Worked in rounds using sport weight yarn, it features a lacy pattern of cluster stitches and a scalloped edging. The traditional look of this sweet wrap will make it a treasure for many generations.

Finished Size: Approximately 36" x 36"

MATERIALS

Sport Weight Yarn, approximately:

Color A (Pink) - 1½ ounces, (40 grams, 140 yards)
Color B (Peach) - 2 ounces, (60 grams, 190 yards)
Color C (Yellow) - 3 ounces, (90 grams, 285 yards)
Color D (Green) - 4½ ounces, (130 grams, 425 yards)
Color E (Blue) - 5½ ounces, (160 grams, 520 yards)
Color F (Lavender) - 6 ounces, (170 grams, 565 yards)

Crochet hook, size H (5.00 mm) **or** size needed for gauge

Note: Entire Afghan is worked holding two strands of yarn together.

GAUGE: Rnds 1-4 = 4½"

PATTERN STITCHES

CORNER (uses one sc)
YO, insert hook in **next** sc, YO and pull up a loop, YO and draw through 2 loops on hook, (YO, insert hook in **same** st, YO and pull up a loop, YO and draw through 2 loops on hook) twice, YO and draw through all 4 loops on hook, ch 3, ★ YO, insert hook in **same** st, YO and pull up a loop, YO and draw through 2 loops on hook; repeat from ★ 2 times **more**, YO and draw through all 4 loops on hook.

BEGINNING CLUSTER (uses next 2 sc)
Ch 2, turn; ★ YO, insert hook in **next** sc, YO and pull up a loop, YO and draw through 2 loops on hook; repeat from ★ once **more**, YO and draw through all 3 loops on hook.

CLUSTER (uses next 3 sc)
★ YO insert hook in **next** sc, YO and pull up a loop, YO and draw through 2 loops on hook; repeat from ★ 2 times **more**; YO and draw through all 4 loops on hook ***(Figs. 16a & b, page 120)***.

Rnd 1 (Right side)**:** Holding two strands of Color A together, ch 4, 3 dc in fourth ch from hook, ch 2, (4 dc in same ch, ch 2) 3 times; join with slip st to top of beginning ch-4: 4 ch-2 sps.

Note: Loop a short piece of yarn around any stitch to mark last round as **right** side.

Rnd 2: Ch 1, turn; (3 sc in next ch-2 sp, sc in next 4 sts) around; join with slip st to first sc: 28 sc.

Rnd 3: Work beginning Cluster, ch 2, work Cluster, ch 2, work Corner, ch 2, ★ (work Cluster, ch 2) twice, work Corner, ch 2; repeat from ★ around; join with slip st to top of beginning Cluster: 8 Clusters and 4 Corners.

Rnd 4: Ch 1, turn; 2 sc in first ch-2 sp, sc in next st, 3 sc in corner ch-3 sp, sc in next st, ★ (2 sc in next ch-2 sp, sc in next st) across to next corner ch-3 sp, 3 sc in corner ch-3 sp, sc in next st; repeat from ★ 2 times **more**, (2 sc in next ch-2 sp, sc in next st) across; join with slip st to first sc changing to one strand Color A and one strand Color B ***(Fig. 30b, page 124)***: 52 sc.

Rnd 5: Work beginning Cluster, ch 2, (work Cluster, ch 2) twice, work Corner, ch 2, ★ (work Cluster, ch 2) across to center sc of next corner, work Corner, ch 2; repeat from ★ 2 times **more**, work Cluster, ch 2; join with slip st to top of beginning Cluster: 16 Clusters and 4 Corners.

Rnd 6: Ch 1, turn; 2 sc in first ch-2 sp, sc in next st, 2 sc in next ch-2 sp, sc in next st, 3 sc in corner ch-3 sp, sc in next st, ★ (2 sc in next ch-2 sp, sc in next st) across to next corner ch-3 sp, 3 sc in corner ch-3 sp, sc in next st; repeat from ★ 2 times **more**, (2 sc in next ch-2 sp, sc in next st) across; join with slip st to first sc changing to two strands Color B: 76 sc.

Rnd 7: Work beginning Cluster, ch 2, ★ (work Cluster, ch 2) across to next corner sc, work Corner, ch 2; repeat from ★ 3 times **more**, (work Cluster, ch 2) across; join with slip st to top of beginning Cluster: 24 Clusters and 4 Corners.

Rnd 8: Ch 1, turn; 2 sc in first ch-2 sp, sc in next st, ★ (2 sc in next ch-2 sp, sc in next st) across to next corner ch-3 sp, 3 sc in corner ch-3 sp, sc in next st; repeat from ★ 3 times **more**, (2 sc in next ch-2 sp, sc in next st) across; join with slip st to first sc: 100 sc.

Rnds 9 and 10: Repeat Rnds 7 and 8 changing to one strand Color B and one strand Color C when joining at end of Rnd 10: 124 sc.

Rnds 11 and 12: Repeat Rnds 7 and 8 changing to two strands Color C when joining at end of Rnd 12: 148 sc.

Rnds 13-16: Repeat Rnds 7 and 8 twice changing to one strand Color C and one strand Color D when joining at end of Rnd 16: 196 sc.

Rnds 17-20: Repeat Rnds 7 and 8 twice changing to two strands Color D when joining at end of Rnd 20: 244 sc.

Rnds 21-24: Repeat Rnds 7 and 8 twice changing to one strand Color D and one strand Color E when joining at end of Rnd 24: 292 sc.

Rnds 25 and 26: Repeat Rnds 7 and 8 changing to two strands Color E when joining at end of Rnd 26: 316 sc.
Rnds 27-30: Repeat Rnds 7 and 8 twice changing to one strand Color E and one strand Color F when joining at end of Rnd 30: 364 sc.
Rnds 31 and 32: Repeat Rnds 7 and 8 changing to two strands Color F when joining at end of Rnd 32: 388 sc.
Rnds 33-36: Repeat Rnds 7 and 8 twice changing to one strand Color F and one strand Color A when joining at end of Rnd 36: 436 sc.

Rnd 37: Ch 3, turn; 4 dc in first sc, skip next sc, slip st in next sc, ★ skip next sc, (5 dc in next sc, skip next sc, slip st in next sc, skip next sc) across to next corner sc, 7 dc in corner sc, skip next 2 sc, slip st in next sc; repeat from ★ 3 times **more**, skip next sc, (5 dc in next sc, skip next sc, slip st in next sc, skip next sc) across; join with slip st to top of beginning ch-3, finish off.

MIMOSA BLOSSOMS

Especially easy to make, this afghan brings to mind images of wispy mimosa blossoms. The throw is created entirely with single crochet stitches, using long single crochets to form the blooms.

Finished Size: Approximately 47" x 59"

MATERIALS

Worsted Weight Yarn, approximately:
86 ounces, (2,440 grams, 4,015 yards)
Crochet hook, size K (6.50 mm) **or** size needed for gauge

Note: Entire Afghan is worked holding two strands of yarn together.

GAUGE: 9 sc and 12 rows = 4"

Ch 106 **loosely**.

Row 1 (Right side)**:** Sc in second ch from hook and in each ch across: 105 sc.

Note: Loop a short piece of yarn around any stitch to mark last row as **right** side.

Rows 2-4: Ch 1, turn; sc in each sc across.

Note: To work **long sc**, insert hook in st indicated, YO and pull up a loop even with last st made, YO and draw through both loops on hook.

Row 5: Ch 1, turn; sc in first sc, ★ work long sc in sc 3 rows **below** and 3 sts to the left of next sc ***(Fig. 20a, page 121)***, skip sc under long sc, sc in next sc, work 3 long sc in same st as first long sc, skip 3 sc under long sc, sc in next sc, work long sc in same st as first long sc ***(Fig. 20b, page 121)***, skip sc under long sc, sc in next sc; repeat from ★ across: 13 Mimosa Blossoms.

Rows 6-10: Ch 1, turn; sc in each st across.

Row 11: Ch 1, turn; sc in first 5 sc, work long sc in sc 3 rows **below** and 3 sts to the left of next sc, skip sc under long sc, sc in next sc, work 3 long sc in same st as first long sc, skip 3 sc under long sc, sc in next sc, work long sc in same st as first long sc, skip sc under long sc, ★ sc in next sc, work long sc in sc 3 rows **below** and 3 sts to the left of next sc, skip sc under long sc, sc in next sc, work 3 long sc in same st as first long sc, skip 3 sc under long sc, sc in next sc, work long sc in same st as first long sc, skip sc under long sc; repeat from ★ across to last 5 sc, sc in last 5 sc: 12 Mimosa Blossoms.

Rows 12-16: Ch 1, turn; sc in each st across.

Repeat Rows 5-16 until Afghan measures approximately 58 1/2" from beginning ch, ending by working Row 7. Finish off.

EDGING

With **right** side facing and working in free loops of beginning ch ***(Fig. 29b, page 124)***, join yarn with slip st in first ch; ch 1, sc in same ch and in each ch across; finish off.

OCEAN BREEZE

A blanket of graceful shell stitches, this lovely afghan will chase away the chill from a cool ocean breeze. A repeated pattern and a simple edging make this wrap quick to complete.

Finished Size: Approximately 49" x 65"

MATERIALS

Worsted Weight Yarn, approximately:
47 ounces, (1,330 grams, 3,225 yards)
Crochet hook, size P (10.00 mm) or size needed for gauge

Note: Entire Afghan is worked holding two strands of yarn together.

GAUGE: One Shell = 2" and 4 rows = $3^1/2$"

Note: To work **Shell**, (sc, ch 3, 4 dc) in st indicated.

Ch 94 **loosely**.

Row 1 (Right side)**:** Work Shell in second ch from hook, (skip next 3 chs, work Shell in next ch) across to last 4 chs, skip next 3 chs, sc in last ch: 23 Shells.

Note: Loop a short piece of yarn around any stitch to mark last row as **right** side.

Row 2: Ch 6 **(counts as first dc plus ch 3)**, turn; skip next 4 dc, sc in next ch, ★ ch 3, skip next 4 dc, sc in next ch; repeat from ★ across: 23 sc.

Row 3: Ch 1, turn; work Shell in first sc and in each sc across to last dc, sc in last dc: 23 Shells.

Repeat Rows 2 and 3 until Afghan measures approximately 63" from beginning ch, ending by working Row 2; do **not** finish off.

EDGING

Rnd 1: Ch 1, turn; 3 sc in first sc, work 90 sc evenly spaced across to last dc, 3 sc in last dc; work 138 sc evenly spaced across end of rows; working in free loops of beginning ch ***(Fig. 29b, page 124)***, 3 sc in first ch, work 90 sc evenly spaced across to next corner ch, 3 sc in corner ch; work 138 sc evenly spaced across end of rows; join with slip st to first sc: 468 sc.

Rnd 2: Ch 1, do **not** turn; sc in same st, ch 3, ★ skip next sc, sc in next 2 sc, ch 3; repeat from ★ around to last 2 sc, skip next sc, sc in last sc; join with slip st to first sc, finish off.

FANCIFUL FANS

Rows of delicate scallops resemble Victorian fans on this fanciful throw, which is worked in bright pastel worsted weight yarns. The timeless pattern is enhanced with tasseled fringe.

Finished Size: Approximately 48½" x 62"

MATERIALS

Worsted Weight Yarn, approximately:
- MC (Ecru) - 24 ounces, (680 grams, 1,575 yards)
- Color A (Yellow) - 12 ounces, (340 grams, 790 yards)
- Color B (Pink) - 12 ounces, (340 grams, 790 yards)
- Color C (Blue) - 11 ounces, (310 grams, 725 yards)

Crochet hook, size N (9.00 mm) **or** size needed for gauge

Note: Entire Afghan is worked holding two strands of yarn together.

GAUGE: In pattern, 2 repeats (24 sts) = 8¾" and 8 rows = 5¼"

STRIPE SEQUENCE

One row **each** MC ***(Fig. 30a, page 124)***, ★ Color A, MC, Color B, MC, Color C; repeat from ★ throughout.

With MC, ch 138 **loosely**.

Row 1: Dc in sixth ch from hook **(5 skipped chs count as first dc plus ch 2)**, skip next 3 chs, sc in next 5 chs, ★ skip next 3 chs, dc in next ch, (ch 2, dc in same st) twice, skip next 3 chs, sc in next 5 chs; repeat from ★ across to last 4 chs, skip next 3 chs, (dc, ch 2, dc) in last ch: 22 ch-2 sps.

Row 2 (Right side)**:** Ch 3 **(counts as first dc, now and throughout)**, turn; 4 dc in first ch-2 sp, skip next 2 sts, sc in next 3 sc, 4 dc in next ch-2 sp, dc in next dc, ★ 4 dc in next ch-2 sp, skip next 2 sts, sc in next 3 sc, 4 dc in next ch-2 sp, dc in next dc; repeat from ★ across: 133 sts.

Note: Loop a short piece of yarn around any stitch to mark last row as **right** side.

Row 3: Ch 1, turn; sc in first 3 dc, skip next 3 sts, dc in next sc, (ch 2, dc in same st) twice, ★ skip next 3 sts, sc in next 5 dc, skip next 3 sts, dc in next sc, (ch 2, dc in same st) twice; repeat from ★ across to last 6 sts, skip next 3 sts, sc in last 3 dc: 22 ch-2 sps.

Row 4: Ch 1, turn; sc in first 2 sc, 4 dc in next ch-2 sp, dc in next dc, 4 dc in next ch-2 sp, ★ skip next 2 sts, sc in next 3 sc, 4 dc in next ch-2 sp, dc in next dc, 4 dc in next ch-2 sp; repeat from ★ across to last 4 sts, skip next 2 sts, sc in last 2 sc: 133 sts.

Row 5: Ch 5 **(counts as first dc plus ch 2, now and throughout)**, turn; dc in same st, skip next 3 sts, sc in next 5 dc, ★ skip next 3 sts, dc in next sc, (ch 2, dc in same st) twice, skip next 3 sts, sc in next 5 dc; repeat from ★ across to last 4 sts, skip next 3 sts, (dc, ch 2, dc) in last sc: 22 ch-2 sps.

Row 6: Ch 3, turn; 4 dc in first ch-2 sp, skip next 2 sts, sc in next 3 sc, 4 dc in next ch-2 sp, dc in next dc, ★ 4 dc in next ch-2 sp, skip next 2 sts, sc in next 3 sc, 4 dc in next ch-2 sp, dc in next dc; repeat from ★ across: 133 sts.

Repeat Rows 3-6 until Afghan measures approximately 62" from beginning ch, ending by working Row 3.

Finish off.

Edging - First Side: With **right** side of long edge facing, join MC with sc in right corner ***(see Joining With Sc, page 124)***; sc evenly across end of rows; finish off.

Edging - Second Side: Work same as First Side.

With MC and using twelve 18" strands, add fringe across short edges of Afghan ***(Figs. 33a & c, page 126)***.

SOFT SCALLOPS

This pretty afghan can double as an elegant accent as well as a cuddly cover-up. Its soothing wave pattern is created using double crochet, single crochet, and chain stitches. A scalloped shell edging completes the soft wrap.

Finished Size: Approximately 51" x 72"

MATERIALS

Worsted Weight Yarn, approximately:
MC (Peach) - 39 ounces, (1,110 grams, 2,675 yards)
CC (Ecru) - 33 ounces, (940 grams, 2,265 yards)
Crochet hook, size P (10.00 mm) **or** size needed for gauge

Note: Entire Afghan is worked holding two strands of yarn together.

GAUGE: 9 sts and 4 rows = $4^{1}/_{2}$"

With CC, ch 103 **loosely**.

Row 1: Dc in fourth ch from hook, hdc in next 2 chs, sc in next 3 chs, hdc in next 2 chs, ★ dc in next 3 chs, hdc in next 2 chs, sc in next 3 chs, hdc in next 2 chs; repeat from ★ across to last 2 chs, dc in last 2 chs changing to MC in last dc ***(Fig. 30a, page 124)***: 101 sts.

Note: To work **Shell**, 7 tr in st indicated.

Row 2 (Right side)**:** Ch 1, turn; sc in first 2 dc, skip next 3 sts, work Shell in next sc, ★ skip next 3 sts, sc in next 3 dc, skip next 3 sts, work Shell in next sc; repeat from ★ across to last 5 sts, skip next 3 sts, sc in last 2 sts: 10 Shells.

Note: Loop a short piece of yarn around any stitch to mark last row as **right** side.

Row 3: Ch 3 **(counts as first dc, now and throughout)**, turn; dc in next sc and in each st across changing to CC in last dc: 101 dc.

Row 4: Ch 4, turn; 3 tr in same st, skip next 3 dc, sc in next 3 dc, ★ skip next 3 dc, work Shell in next dc, skip next 3 dc, sc in next 3 dc; repeat from ★ across to last 4 dc, skip next 3 dc, 4 tr in last dc: 9 Shells.

Row 5: Ch 3, turn; dc in next tr and in each st across changing to MC in last dc: 101 dc.

Row 6: Ch 1, turn; sc in first 2 dc, skip next 3 dc, work Shell in next dc, ★ skip next 3 dc, sc in next 3 dc, skip next 3 dc, work Shell in next dc; repeat from ★ across to last 5 dc, skip next 3 dc, sc in last 2 dc: 10 Shells.

Repeat Rows 3-6 until Afghan measures approximately 66" from beginning ch, ending by working Row 3.

Last Row: Ch 3, turn; dc in next dc, hdc in next 2 dc, sc in next 3 dc, hdc in next 2 dc, ★ dc in next 3 dc, hdc in next 2 dc, sc in next 3 dc, hdc in next 2 dc; repeat from ★ across to last 2 dc, dc in last 2 dc; finish off.

EDGING

Rnd 1: With **right** side facing, join MC with sc in top **right** corner ***(see Joining With Sc, page 124)***; 2 sc in same st, sc in each st across to last dc, 3 sc in last dc; work 144 sc evenly spaced across end of rows; working in free loops of beginning ch ***(Fig. 29b, page 124)***, 3 sc in ch at base of first st, sc in each ch across to last ch, 3 sc in last ch; work 144 sc evenly spaced across end of rows; join with slip st to first sc: 498 sc.

Rnd 2: Slip st in next sc, ch 4, (dc, ch 1, tr) in same st, (ch 1, dc in same st) twice, ★ † skip next 2 sc, sc in next 2 sc, [skip next sc, (dc, ch 1, tr, ch 1, dc) in next sc, skip next sc, sc in next 2 sc] across to within 2 sc of corner sc, skip next 2 sts †, (dc in corner sc, ch 1) twice, tr in same st, (ch 1, dc in same st) twice; repeat from ★ 2 times **more**, then repeat from † to † once; join with slip st to third ch of beginning ch-4, finish off.

SIMPLICITY

You just repeat two simple stitches to fashion the allover pattern on this comfy throw. Generous fringe and fluffy yarn make the afghan a joy to use every day.

Finished Size: Approximately 45" x 60$^{1}/_{2}$"

MATERIALS

Worsted Weight Brushed Acrylic Yarn, approximately:
47 ounces, (1,330 grams, 3,625 yards)
Crochet hook, size P (10.00 mm) **or** size needed for gauge

Note: Entire Afghan is worked holding two strands of yarn together.

GAUGE: Decrease, (ch 1, decrease) 5 times and 11 rows = 5"

PATTERN STITCHES

BEGINNING DECREASE

Insert hook in first sc, YO and pull up a loop, insert hook in next ch-1 sp, YO and pull up a loop, YO and draw through all 3 loops on hook **(counts as one sc)**.

DECREASE

Insert hook in next sc, YO and pull up a loop, insert hook in next ch-1 sp, YO and pull up a loop, YO and draw through all 3 loops on hook **(counts as one sc)**.

Ch 100 **loosely**.

Row 1 (Right side)**:** Insert hook in second ch from hook, YO and pull up a loop, insert hook in next ch, YO and pull up a loop, YO and draw through all 3 loops on hook, ch 1, ★ (insert hook in **next** ch, YO and pull up a loop) twice, YO and draw through all 3 loops on hook, ch 1; repeat from ★ across to last ch, sc in last ch: 49 ch-1 sps.

Note: Loop a short piece of yarn around any stitch to mark last row as **right** side.

Row 2: Ch 1, turn; work beginning decrease, ch 1, (decrease, ch 1) across to last sc, sc in last sc.

Repeat Row 2 until Afghan measures approximately 60$^{1}/_{2}$" from beginning ch, ending by working a **right** side row. Finish off.

Using three 16" strands, add fringe across short edges of Afghan ***(Figs. 33a & c, page 126)***.

STARS FOR BABY

Your little one will look like an angel beneath this blanket of stars! Worked in variegated pastels, the wrap is perfect for either boys or girls. White fringe adds a dreamy finish.

Finished Size: Approximately 38" x 45"

MATERIALS

Worsted Weight Yarn, approximately:
MC (White) - 33 ounces, (940 grams, 1,225 yards)
CC (Variegated) - 29 ounces, (820 grams, 1,075 yards)
Crochet hook, size P (10.00 mm) **or** size needed for gauge

Note: Each row is worked across length of Afghan holding one strand MC and one strand CC yarn together.

GAUGE: 7 Stars = 5" and 5 rows = 4"

PATTERN STITCHES

BEGINNING STAR STITCH

Ch 3, turn; pull up a loop in second ch from hook and in next ch, pull up a loop in next st and in next ch-1 sp, YO and draw through all 5 loops on hook.

STAR STITCH

Ch 1, pull up a loop in ch-1 just made and in last loop on back of last Star St ***(Fig. 25, page 122)***, pull up a loop in next st and in next ch-1 sp, YO and draw through all 5 loops on hook.

ENDING STAR STITCH

Ch 1, pull up a loop in ch-1 just made and in last loop on back of last Star St ***(Fig. 25, page 122)***, pull up a loop in next st and in top of turning ch, YO and draw through all 5 loops on hook.

Ch 129 **loosely**.

Row 1 (Right side)**:** Pull up a loop in second ch from hook and in next 3 chs, YO and draw through all 5 loops on hook, ★ ch 1, pull up a loop in ch-1 just made and in last loop on back of last st ***(Fig. 25, page 122)***, pull up a loop in next 2 chs, YO and draw through all 5 loops on hook; repeat from ★ across.

Note: Loop a short piece of yarn around any stitch to mark last row as **right** side.

Row 2: Work beginning Star St, work Star Sts across to last st, work ending Star St: 63 Star Sts.

Repeat Row 2 until Afghan measures approximately 37" from beginning ch, ending by working a **wrong** side row.

Last Row: Work beginning Star St, work Star Sts across to last st, work ending Star St, ch 1; finish off.

With MC and using six 15" strands, add fringe across short edges of Afghan ***(Figs. 33b & d, page 126)***.

DELICATE SHELLS

Crocheted with brushed acrylic yarn, this delicate afghan combines ecru and pastel variegated yarns in a profusion of shell stitches. Surrounded by its lacy softness, you'll be lulled into a tranquil afternoon nap.

Finished Size: Approximately 47" x 63$^1/_2$"

MATERIALS

Worsted Weight Brushed Acrylic Yarn, approximately:
MC (Variegated) - 20 ounces, (570 grams, 1,545 yards)
CC (Ecru) - 18 ounces, (510 grams, 1,390 yards)
Crochet hook, size N (9.00 mm) **or** size needed for gauge

Note: Entire Afghan is worked holding two strands of yarn together.

GAUGE: Dc, (Shell, dc) twice = 4"

With CC, ch 136 **loosely**.

Row 1 (Right side)**:** Dc in sixth ch from hook, ★ ch 1, skip next ch, dc in next ch; repeat from ★ across changing to MC in last dc ***(Fig. 30a, page 124)***: 66 sps.

Note: Loop a short piece of yarn around any stitch to mark last row as **right** side.

Row 2: Ch 1, turn; sc in first dc, ch 1, (sc in next dc, ch 1) across, skip next ch, sc in next ch.

Note: To work **Shell**, dc in next ch-1 sp, ch 3, work 3 dc around post of dc just made ***(Fig. 17, page 120)***.

Row 3: Ch 3, turn; ★ skip next ch-1 sp, work Shell, skip next sc, dc in next sc; repeat from ★ across changing to CC in last dc: 22 Shells.

Row 4: Ch 5, turn; skip next 3 dc, sc in next ch, ch 2, ★ dc in next dc (between Shells), ch 2, skip next 3 dc, sc in next ch, ch 2; repeat from ★ across, dc in top of turning ch.

Row 5: Ch 4, turn; (dc in next sp, ch 1) twice, ★ dc in next dc, ch 1, (dc in next sp, ch 1) twice; repeat from ★ across, dc in third ch of turning ch changing to MC.

Repeat Rows 2-5 until Afghan measures approximately 61" from beginning ch, ending by working Row 5; do **not** change to MC at end of last row and do **not** finish off.

EDGING

Rnd 1: Ch 1, do **not** turn; work 157 sc evenly spaced across end of rows; working in free loops of beginning ch ***(Fig. 29b, page 124)***, 3 sc in first ch, 2 sc in next ch, sc in next 129 chs, 2 sc in next ch, 3 sc in next ch; work 157 sc evenly spaced across end of rows; working across sts of last row, 3 sc in third ch of beginning ch-4, 2 sc in first ch-1 sp, sc in each dc and in each ch-1 sp across to last ch-1 sp, 2 sc in last ch-1 sp, 3 sc in last dc; join with slip st to first sc, finish off: 592 sc.

Rnd 2: With **right** side facing, join MC with slip st in any corner sc; ch 3, 4 dc in same st, skip next sc, sc in next sc, (skip next 2 sc, 5 dc in next sc, skip next 2 sc, sc in next sc) across to within one sc of next corner sc, ★ 5 dc in corner sc, skip next sc, sc in next sc, (skip next 2 sc, 5 dc in next sc, skip next 2 sc, sc in next sc) across to within one sc of next corner sc; repeat from ★ around; join with slip st to top of beginning ch-3, finish off.

VICTORIAN LACE

With all the beauty of the Victorian Era, this feminine wrap will capture the hearts of sentimental souls. The afghan is worked in brushed acrylic yarn for an extra downy feel.

Finished Size: Approximately 46" x 66"

MATERIALS

Worsted Weight Brushed Acrylic Yarn, approximately:
45 ounces, (1,280 grams, 3,470 yards)
Crochet hook, size N (9.00 mm) **or** size needed for gauge

Note: Entire Afghan is worked holding two strands of yarn together.

GAUGE: 10 sc = 4" and 10 rows = 6$^1/_2$"
(6$^1/_2$" point to point)

Ch 160 **loosely**.

Row 1 (Right side)**:** Sc in second ch from hook and in next 9 chs, 3 sc in next ch, sc in next 10 chs, ★ skip next 2 chs, sc in next 10 chs, 3 sc in next ch, sc in next 10 chs; repeat from ★ across: 161 sc.

Note: Loop a short piece of yarn around any stitch to mark last row as **right** side.

Rows 2-8: Ch 1, turn; working in Back Loops Only ***(Fig. 28, page 124)***, pull up a loop in first 2 sc, YO and draw through all 3 loops on hook **(counts as one sc)**, sc in next 9 sc, 3 sc in next sc, ★ sc in next 10 sc, skip next 2 sc, sc in next 10 sc, 3 sc in next sc; repeat from ★ 5 times **more**, sc in next 9 sc, pull up a loop in last 2 sc, YO and draw through 3 all loops on hook **(counts as one sc)**: 161 sc.

Note: To work **V-St**, (tr, ch 1, tr) in st or sp indicated.

Row 9: Ch 3, turn; working in Back Loops Only, tr in next sc, skip next 2 sc, (work V-St in next sc, skip next 2 sc) twice, tr in next sc, ch 1, work V-St in next sc, ch 1, tr in next sc, (skip next 2 sc, work V-St in next sc) twice, ★ [YO twice, skip next 2 sc, insert hook in next sc, YO and pull up a loop, (YO and draw through 2 loops on hook) twice] 2 times, YO and draw through all 3 loops on hook, skip next 2 sc, (work V-St in next sc, skip next 2 sc) twice, tr in next sc, ch 1, work V-St in next sc, ch 1, tr in next sc, (skip next 2 sc, work V-St in next sc) twice; repeat from ★ across to last 4 sc, skip next 2 sc, [YO twice, insert hook in next sc, YO and pull up a loop, (YO and draw through 2 loops on hook) twice] 2 times, YO and draw through all 3 loops on hook: 35 V-Sts.

Row 10: Ch 3, turn; working in both loops of tr and in ch-1 sps, tr in first ch-1 sp, work V-St in next 2 ch-1 sps, tr in next tr, ch 1, work V-St in next ch-1 sp, ch 1, tr in next tr, work V-St in next 2 ch-1 sps, ★ [YO twice, insert hook in next ch-1 sp, YO and pull up a loop, (YO and draw through 2 loops on hook) twice] 2 times, YO and draw through all 3 loops on hook, work V-St in next 2 ch-1 sps, tr in next tr, ch 1, work V-St in next ch-1 sp, ch 1, tr in next tr, work V-St in next 2 ch-1 sps; repeat from ★ across to last ch-1 sp, YO twice, insert hook in last ch-1 sp, YO and pull up a loop, (YO and draw through 2 loops on hook) twice, YO twice, insert hook in last tr, YO and pull up a loop, (YO and draw through 2 loops on hook) twice, YO and draw through all 3 loops on hook.

Row 11: Ch 1, turn; working in Back Loops Only of each tr and each ch, pull up a loop in first 2 sts, YO and draw through all 3 loops on hook, sc in next 8 sts, 5 sc in next ch, ★ sc in next 9 sts, skip next st, sc in next 9 sts, 5 sc in next ch; repeat from ★ 5 times **more**, sc in next 8 sts, pull up a loop in last 2 tr, YO and draw through all 3 loops on hook: 161 sc.

Rows 12-98: Repeat Rows 2-11, 8 times; then repeat Rows 2-8 once **more**.

Finish off.

SPRING AWAKENING

Resembling the muted hues found in a spring landscape, the leafy pattern on this plush afghan is worked in double crochet and long double crochet stitches. Single crochet loops, accented with double crochet clusters, complete the irresistible porch-swing companion.

Finished Size: Approximately 45½" x 61"

MATERIALS

Worsted Weight Yarn, approximately:
Color A (Green) - 15½ ounces, (440 grams, 1,020 yards)
Color B (White) - 21 ounces, (600 grams, 1,380 yards)
Color C (Light Green) - 14½ ounces, (410 grams, 955 yards)
Crochet hook, size N (9.00 mm) **or** size needed for gauge

Note: Entire Afghan is worked holding two strands of yarn together.

GAUGE: 12 sts and 7 rows = 5"

STRIPE SEQUENCE

2 Rows of **each** color: Color A ***(Fig. 30a, page 124)***, ★ Color B, Color C, Color A; repeat from ★ 13 times **more**.

With Color A, ch 105 **loosely**.

Row 1 (Right side)**:** Dc in fourth ch from hook **(3 skipped chs count as first dc)** and in next ch, ★ ch 1, skip next ch, dc in next 3 chs; repeat from ★ across: 25 ch-1 sps.

Note: Loop a short piece of yarn around any stitch to mark last row as **right** side.

Row 2: Ch 3 **(counts as first dc, now and throughout)**, turn; dc in next 2 dc, (ch 1, dc in next 3 dc) across.

Note: To work **Long double crochet *(abbreviated Ldc)***, YO, insert hook in ch-1 sp one row **below** next ch-1 sp ***(Fig. 14b, page 120)***, YO and pull up a loop even with last st made, (YO and draw through 2 loops on hook) twice.

Row 3: Ch 4 **(counts as first dc plus ch 1, now and throughout)**, turn; skip next dc, dc in next dc, ★ work Ldc, dc in next dc, ch 1, skip next dc, dc in next dc; repeat from ★ across: 26 ch-1 sps.

Row 4: Ch 4, turn; skip first ch-1 sp, dc in next 3 sts, ★ ch 1, skip next ch-1 sp, dc in next 3 sts; repeat from ★ across to last ch-1 sp, ch 1, skip last ch-1 sp, dc in last dc.

Row 5: Ch 3, turn; work Ldc, dc in next dc, ★ ch 1, skip next dc, dc in next dc, work Ldc, dc in next dc; repeat from ★ across: 25 ch-1 sps.

Row 6: Ch 3, turn; dc in next 2 sts, ★ ch 1, skip next ch-1 sp, dc in next 3 sts; repeat from ★ across.

Rows 7-86: Repeat Rows 3-6, 20 times.

Finish off.

EDGING

Rnd 1: With **right** side facing, join Color B with slip st in first dc on Row 86; ch 1, 3 sc in same st, sc in each dc and in each ch-1 sp across to last dc, 3 sc in last dc; work 143 sc evenly spaced across end of rows; working in free loops of beginning ch ***(Fig. 29b, page 124)***, 3 sc in first ch, sc in next 101 chs, 3 sc in next ch; work 143 sc evenly spaced across end of rows; join with slip st to first sc: 500 sc.

Rnd 2: Ch 1, sc in same st and in each sc around working 3 sc in each corner sc; join with slip st to first sc: 508 sc.

Rnd 3: ★ Ch 2, skip next sc, 3 dc in next sc, ch 2, skip next sc, slip st in next sc, (ch 2, skip next 2 sc, 3 dc in next sc, ch 2, skip next 2 sc, slip st in next sc) across to within one sc of corner sc; repeat from ★ 2 times **more**, ch 2, skip next sc, 3 dc in next sc, ch 2, skip next sc, (slip st in next sc, ch 2, skip next 2 sc, 3 dc in next sc, ch 2, skip next 2 sc) across; join with slip st in same st as joining, finish off.

GENERAL INSTRUCTIONS

YARN

Yarn listed under Materials for each afghan in this book is given in a generic weight. Once you know the weight of the yarn, any brand of the same weight may be used. This enables you to purchase the brand of yarn you like best.

You may wish to purchase a single skein first and crochet a gauge swatch. Compare the way your yarn looks to the photograph to be sure that you will be satisfied with the results. How many skeins to buy depends on the yardage. Ounces and grams will vary from one brand of the same weight to another, but the yardage required will always remain the same provided gauge is met and maintained.

GAUGE

Correct gauge is essential for proper size. Hook size given in instructions is merely a guide and should never be used without first making a sample swatch in the stitch, yarn, and hook specified. Then measure it, counting your stitches and rows or rounds carefully. If your swatch is smaller than specified, try again with a larger size hook; if larger, try again with a smaller size. Keep trying until you find the size that will give you the specified gauge. DO NOT HESITATE TO CHANGE HOOK SIZE TO OBTAIN CORRECT GAUGE.

ABBREVIATIONS

BLO	Back Loop (s) Only
BPdc	Back Post double crochets (s)
BPtr	Back Post treble crochet(s)
CC	Contrasting Color
ch(s)	chain(s)
dc	double crochet(s)
ex LDC	extended Long double crochet(s)
FLO	Front Loop(s) Only
FPdc	Front Post double crochet(s)
FPtr	Front Post treble crochet(s)
hdc	half double crochet(s)
Ldc	Long double crochet(s)
MC	Main Color
mm	millimeters
Rnd(s)	Round(s)
sc	single crochet(s)
sp(s)	space(s)
st(s)	stitch(es)
tr	treble crochet(s)
YO	yarn over

★ — work instructions following ★ as many **more** times as indicated in addition to the first time.

† to †— work all instructions from first † to second † as many times as specified.

( ) or [ ] — work enclosed instructions **as many** times as specified by the number immediately following **or** work all enclosed instructions in the stitch or space indicated **or** contains explanatory remarks.

BASIC STITCH GUIDE

CHAIN

When beginning a row of crochet in a chain, always skip the first chain from the hook, and work into the second chain from hook (for single crochet) or third chain from hook (for half double crochet), etc. ***(Fig. 1)***.

Fig. 1

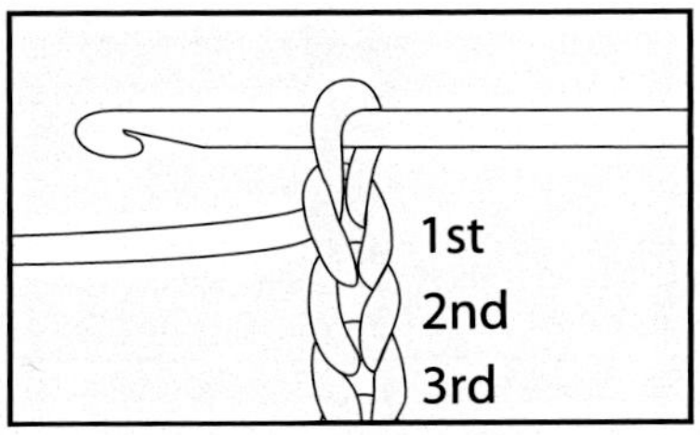

WORKING INTO THE CHAIN

Method 1: Insert hook under top two strands of each chain ***(Fig. 2a)***.
Method 2: Insert hook into back ridge of each chain ***(Fig. 2b)***.

Fig. 2a

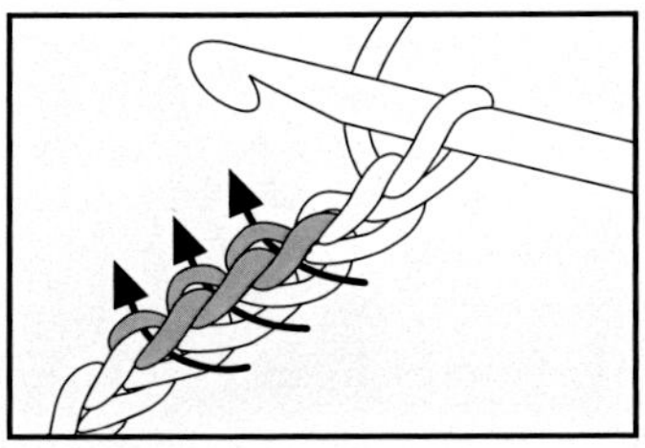

Fig. 2b

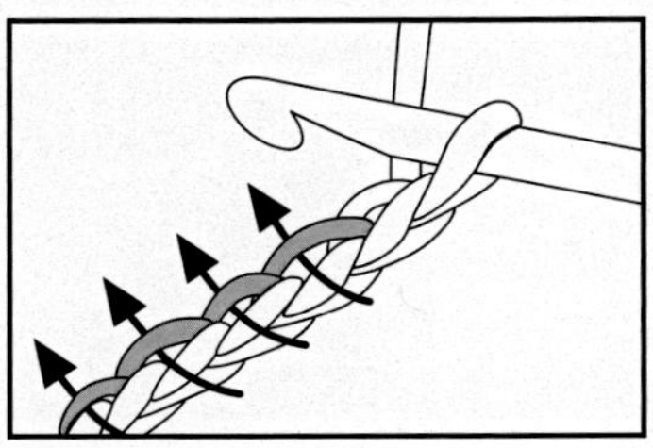

SLIP STITCH

Insert hook in stitch or space indicated, YO and draw through stitch and loop on hook ***(Fig. 3)*** (slip stitch made, abbreviated slip st).

Fig. 3

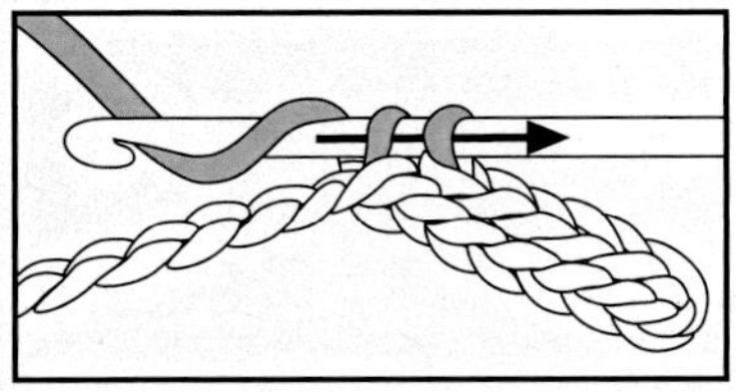

SINGLE CROCHET

Insert hook in stitch or space indicated, YO and pull up a loop (2 loops on hook), YO and draw through both loops on hook ***(Fig. 4)*** **(single crochet made, *abbreviated* sc)**.

Fig. 4

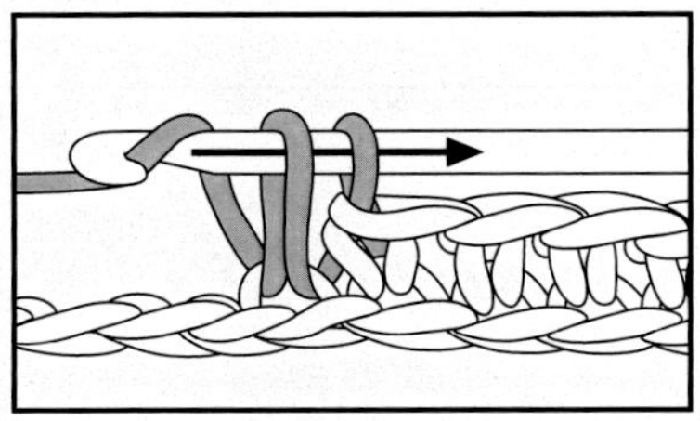

HALF DOUBLE CROCHET

YO, insert hook in stitch or space indicated, YO and pull up a loop (3 loops on hook), YO and draw through all 3 loops on hook ***(Fig. 5)*** **(half double crochet made, *abbreviated* hdc)**.

Fig. 5

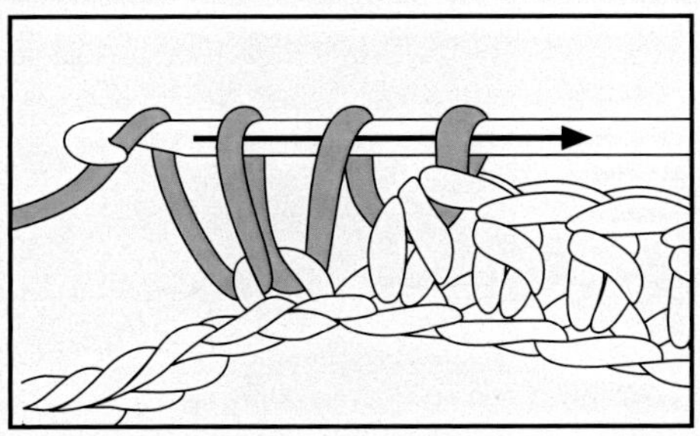

DOUBLE CROCHET

YO, insert hook in stitch or space indicated, YO and pull up a loop (3 loops on hook), YO and draw through 2 loops on hook ***(Fig. 6a)***, YO and draw through remaining 2 loops on hook ***(Fig. 6b)*** **(double crochet made, *abbreviated* dc)**.

Fig. 6a

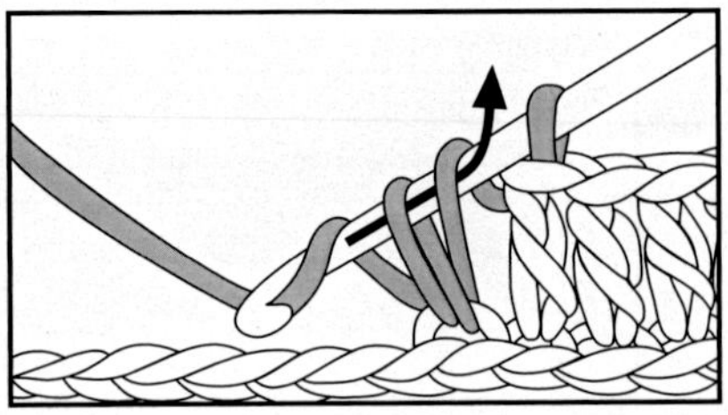

Fig. 6b

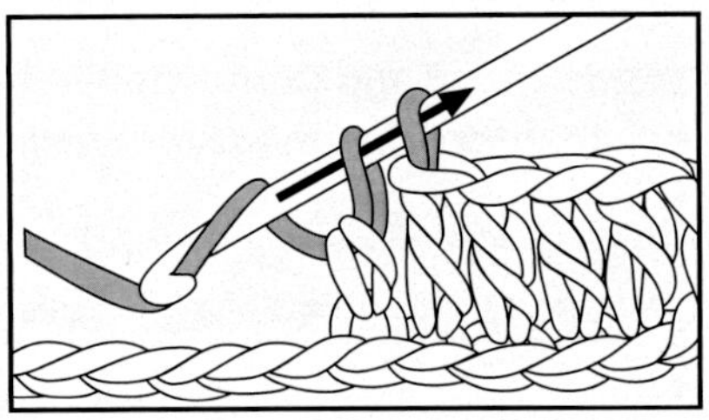

TREBLE CROCHET

YO twice, insert hook in stitch or space indicated, YO and pull up a loop (4 loops on hook) ***(Fig. 7a)***, (YO and draw through 2 loops on hook) 3 times ***(Fig. 7b)*** **(treble crochet made, *abbreviated* tr)**.

Fig. 7a

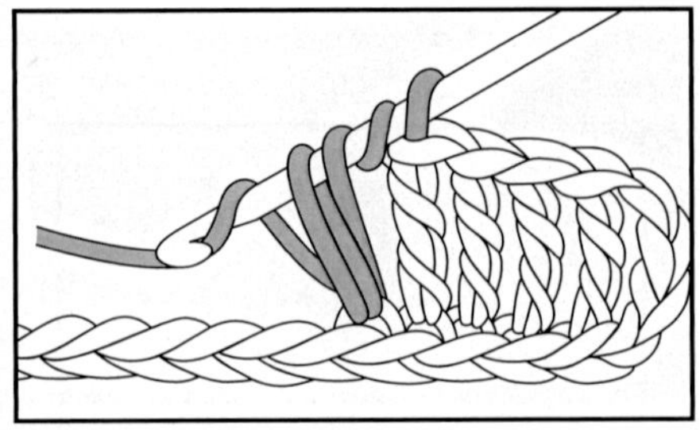

Fig. 7b

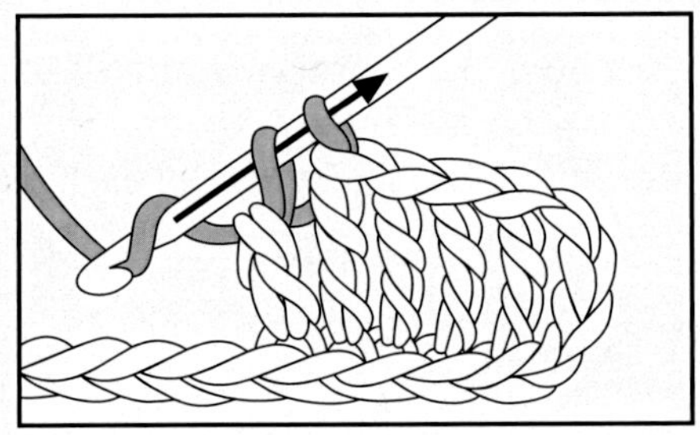

PATTERN STITCHES

POPCORN

Work number of dc specified in stitch or space indicated, drop loop from hook, insert hook in first dc of dc group, hook dropped loop and draw through ***(Figs. 8a & b)***.

Fig. 8a **4-dc Popcorn**

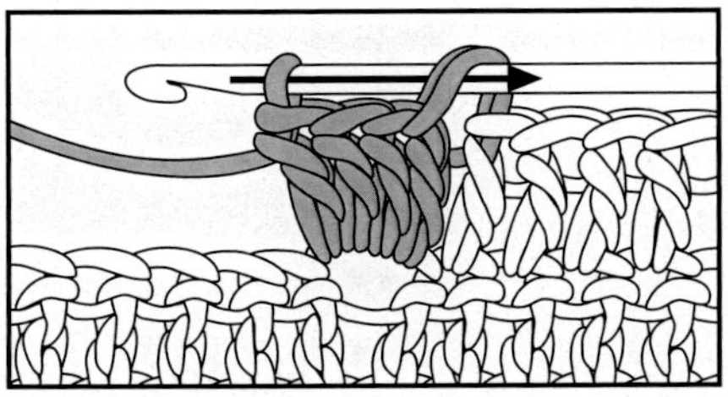

Fig. 8b **5-dc Popcorn**

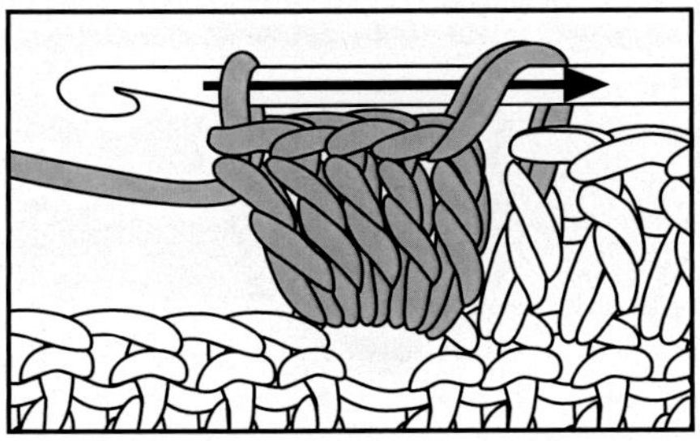

POST STITCH

Work around post of stitch indicated, inserting hook in direction of arrow ***(Fig. 9)***.

Fig. 9

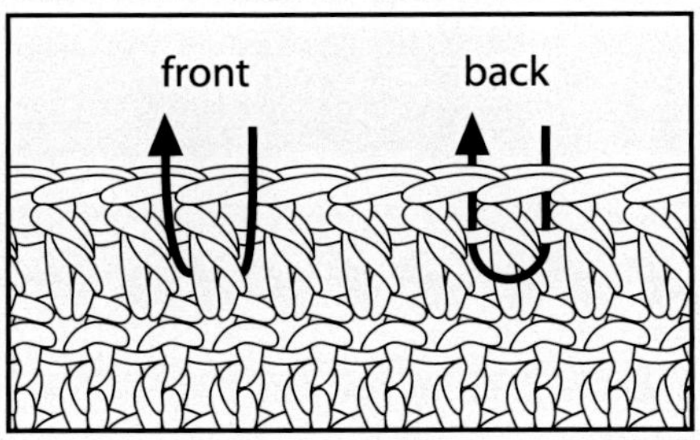

FRONT POST DOUBLE CROCHET

YO, insert hook from **front** to **back** around post of stitch indicated, YO and pull up a loop (3 loops on hook) ***(Fig. 10)***, (YO and draw through 2 loops on hook) twice **(Front Post double crochet made, *abbreviated* FPdc)**.

Fig. 10

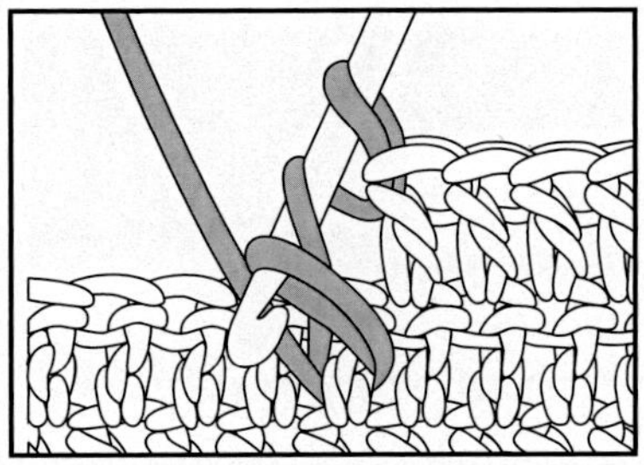

FRONT POST TREBLE CROCHET

YO twice, insert hook from **front** to **back** around post of stitch indicated, YO and pull up a loop (4 loops on hook) ***(Fig, 11)***, (YO and draw through 2 loops on hook) 3 times **(Front Post treble crochet made, *abbreviated* FPtr)**.

Fig. 11

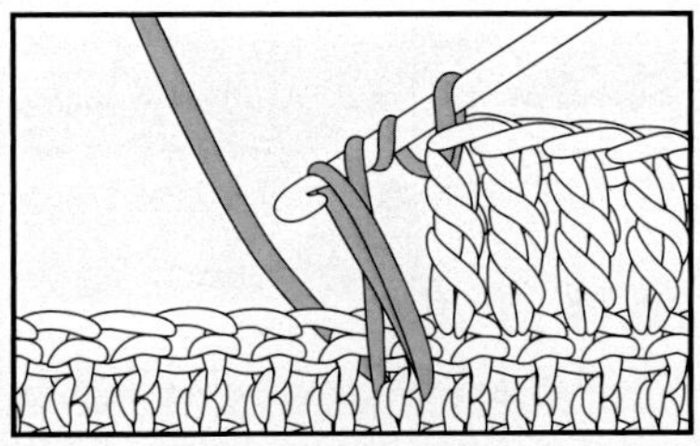

BACK POST DOUBLE CROCHET

YO, insert hook from **back** to **front** around post of stitch indicated, YO and pull up a loop (3 loops on hook) ***(Fig. 12)***, (YO and draw through 2 loops on hook) twice **(Back Post double crochet made, *abbreviated* BPdc)**.

Fig. 12

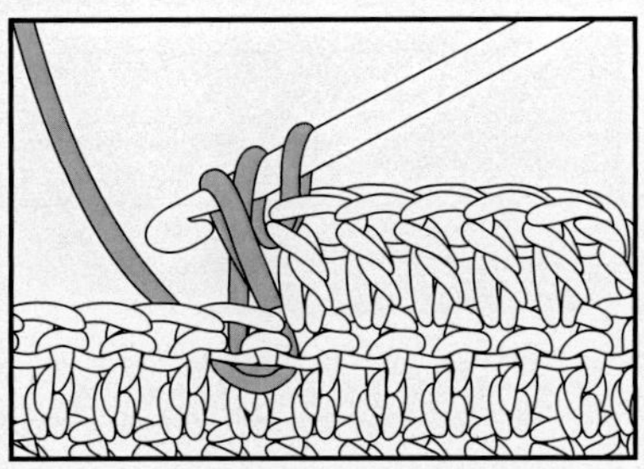

BACK POST TREBLE CROCHET

YO twice, insert hook from **back** to **front** around post of stitch indicated, YO and pull up a loop (4 loops on hook) ***(Fig. 13)***, (YO and draw through 2 loops on hook) 3 times **(Back Post treble crochet made, *abbreviated* BPtr)**.

Fig. 13

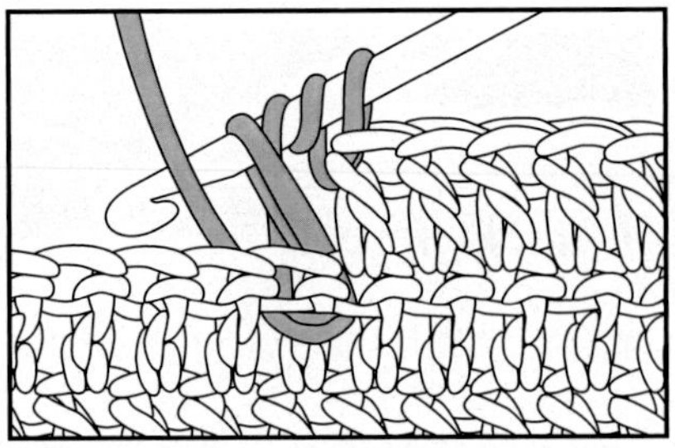

LONG DOUBLE CROCHET

YO, insert hook in stitch ***(Fig. 14a)*** or space ***(Fig. 14b)*** indicated, YO and pull up a loop even with last stitch made (3 loops on hook), (YO and draw through 2 loops on hook) twice.

Fig. 14a

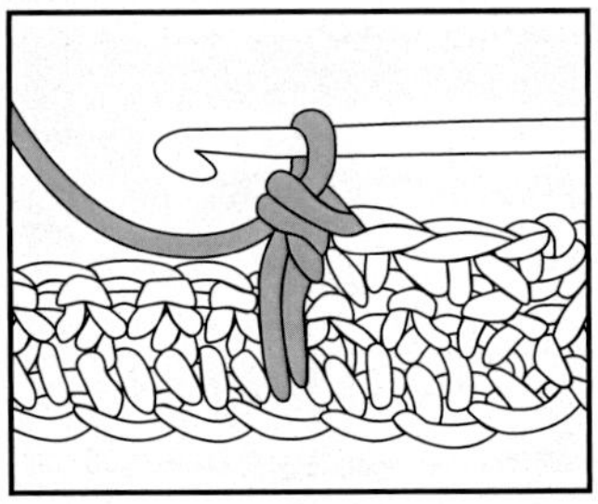

Fig. 14b

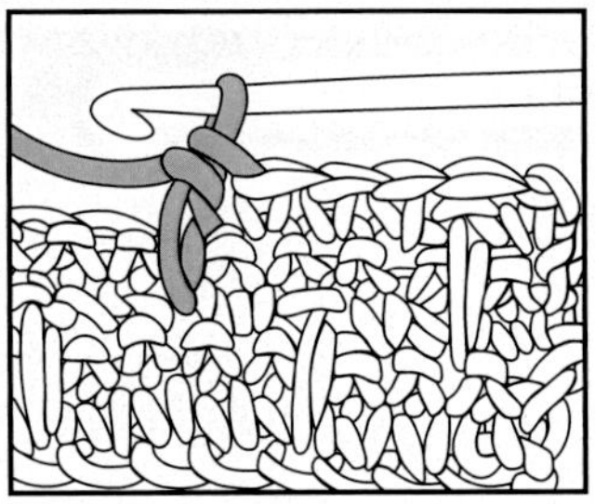

PUFF STITCH

(YO, insert hook in stitch or space indicated, YO and pull up a loop even with stitch on hook) as many times as specified, YO and draw through all loops on hook ***(Fig. 15)***.

Fig. 15

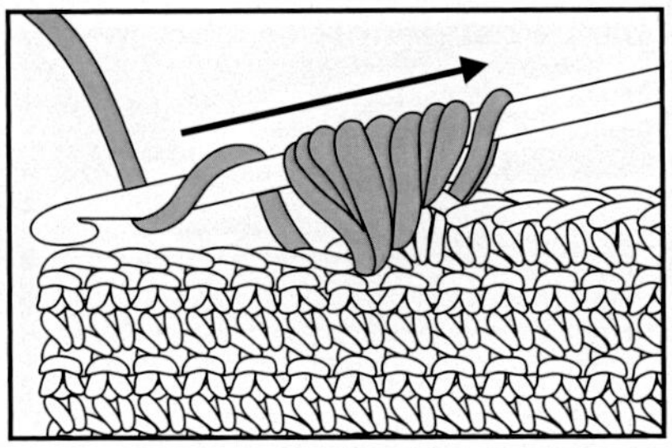

CLUSTER

A Cluster can be worked all in or around the same stitch or space ***(Figs. 16a & b)*** or across several stitches ***(Figs. 16c & d)***.

Fig. 16a

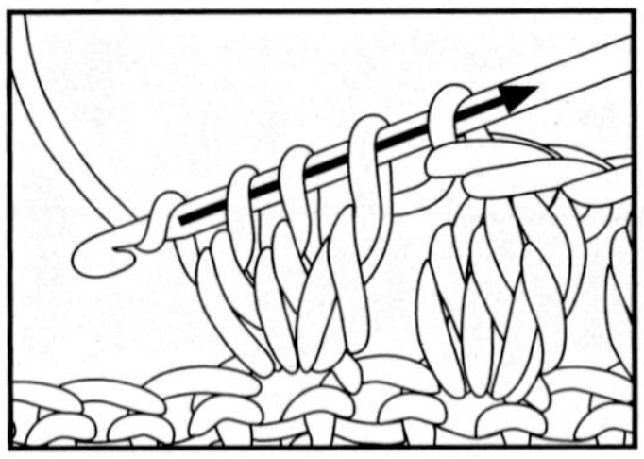

Fig. 16b

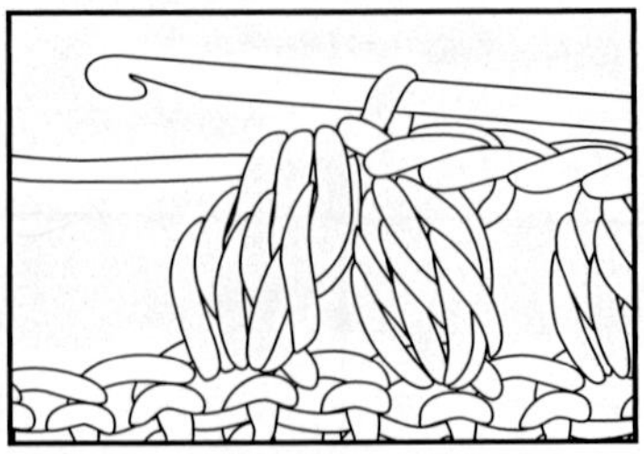

Fig. 16c

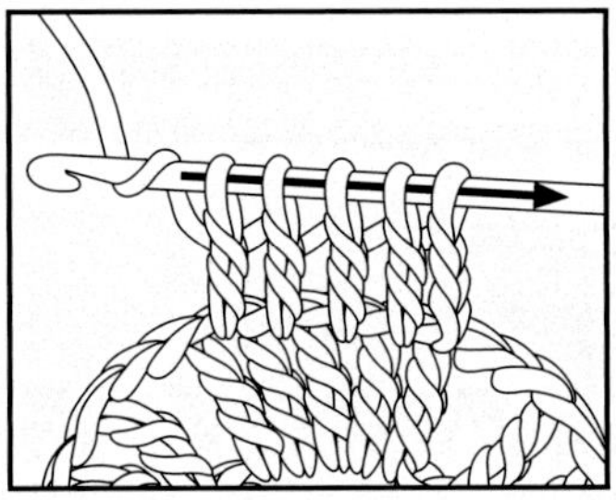

Fig. 16d

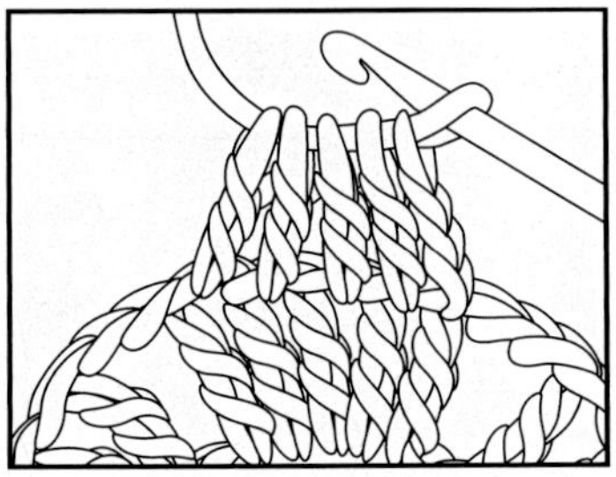

SHELL

Dc in next ch-1 sp, ch 3, work 3 dc around post of dc just made ***(Fig. 17)***.

Fig. 17

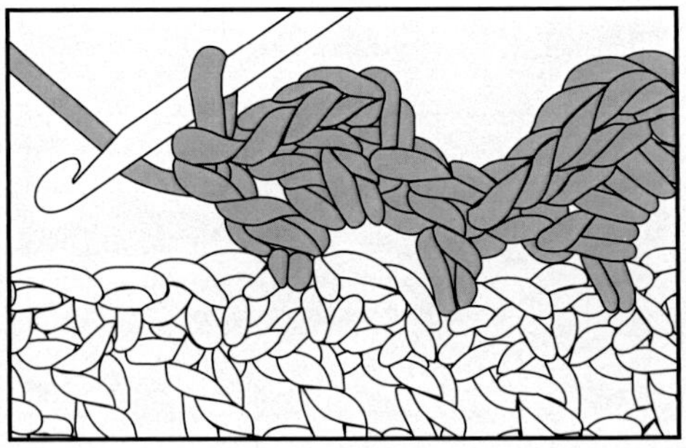

CABLE

Ch 5 **loosely**, slip stitch from **front** to **back** around post of dc 2 rows **below** dc just made ***(Fig. 18a)***, hdc in top loop of each ch just made ***(Fig. 18b)***.

Fig. 18a

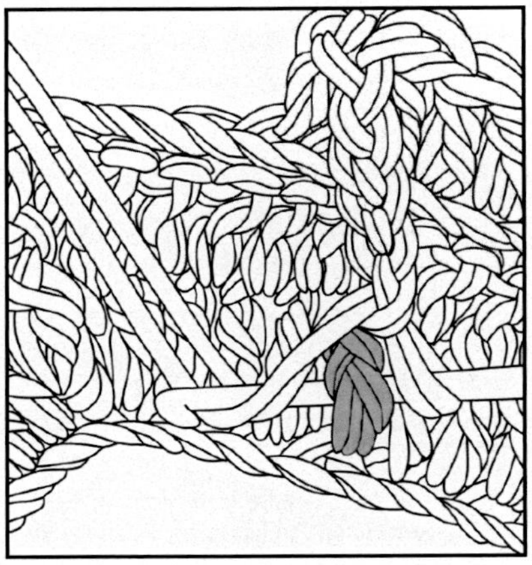

Fig.18b

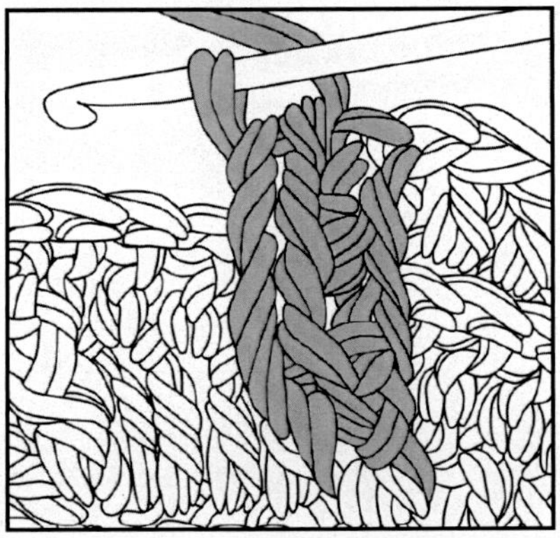

WORKING TO RIGHT OF CABLE

Working to right of previous Cable ***(Fig. 19)***, work Cable.

Fig. 19

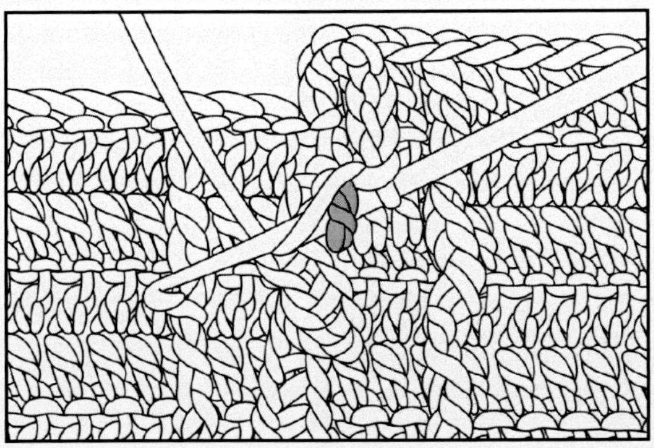

MIMOSA BLOSSOM

Work long sc in sc 3 rows **below** and 3 sts to the left of next sc ***(Fig. 20a)***, skip sc under long sc, sc in next sc, work 3 long sc in same st as first long sc, skip 3 sc under long sc, sc in next sc, work long sc in same st as first long sc ***(Fig. 20b)***, skip sc under long sc.

Fig. 20a

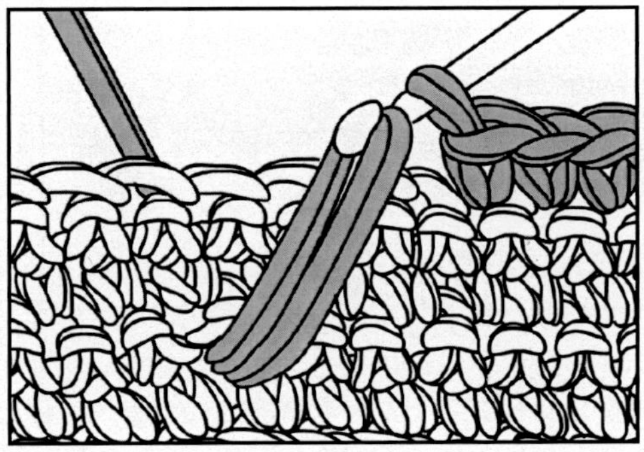

Fig. 20b

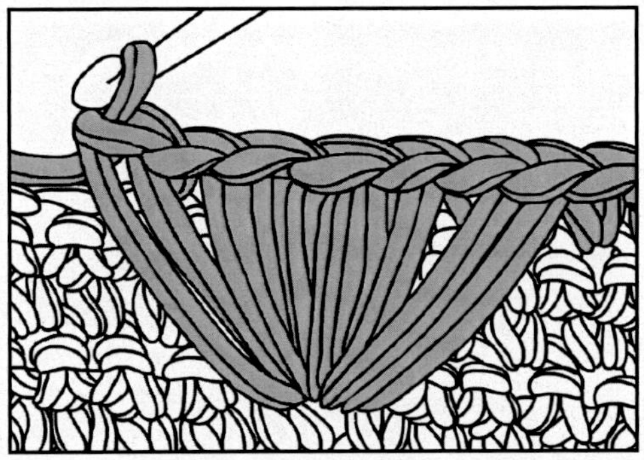

NO SEW JOINING

Hold Squares or Motifs with **wrong** sides together. Slip stitch into space indicated ***(Fig. 21)***.

Fig. 21

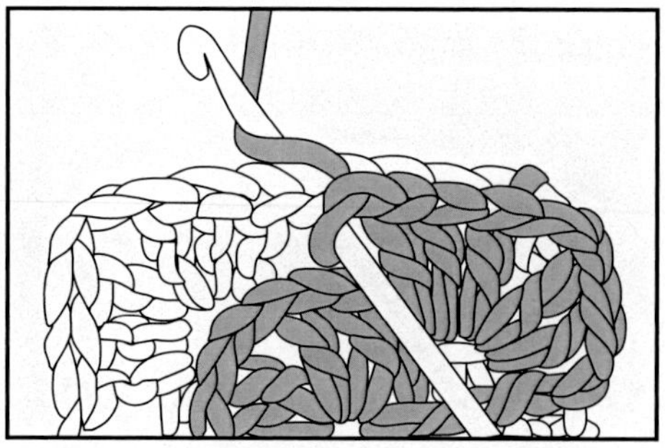

HDC DECREASE

YO, insert hook in next hdc, YO and pull up a loop, YO, skip next hdc, insert hook in next hdc, YO and pull up a loop, YO and draw through all 5 loops on hook (***Fig. 22***, **hdc decrease made**).

Fig. 22

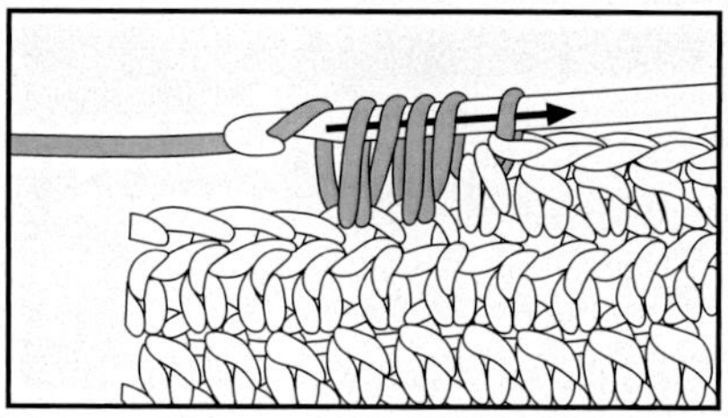

DC DECREASE

YO, insert hook in next st, YO and pull up a loop, YO and draw through 2 loops on hook, YO, skip next st, insert hook in next st, YO and pull up a loop, YO ;md draw through 2 loops on hook, YO and draw through all 3 loops on hook (***Fig. 23***, **dc decrease made**).

Fig. 23

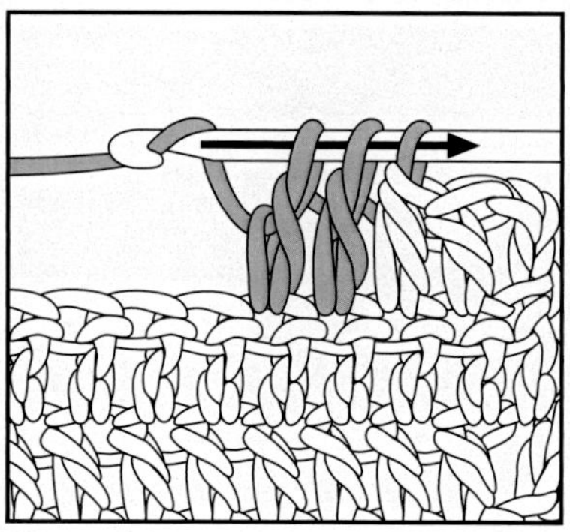

TR DECREASE

YO twice, insert hook in next hdc, YO and pull up a loop, (YO and draw through 2 loops on hook) twice, YO twice, skip next hdc, insert hook in next hdc, YO and pull up a loop, (YO and clrnw through 2 loops on hook) twice, YO and draw through all 3 loops on hook (***Fig. 24***, **tr decrease made**).

Fig. 24

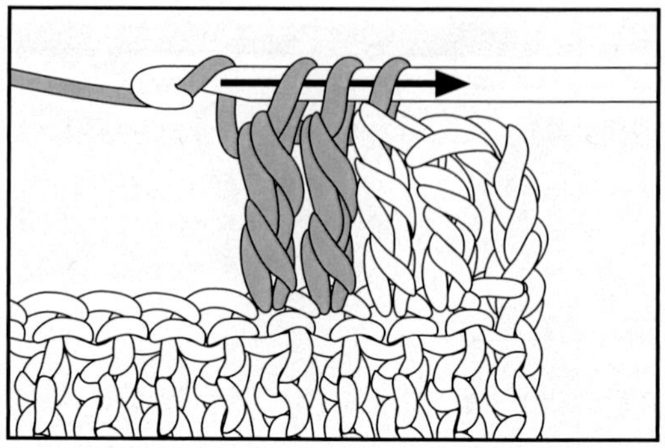

STAR STITCH

Ch 1, pull up a loop in ch-1 just made and in last loop on back of last stitch ***(Fig. 25)***, pull up a loop in next stitch and in next ch-1 sp, YO and drnw through all 5 loops on hook.

Fig. 25

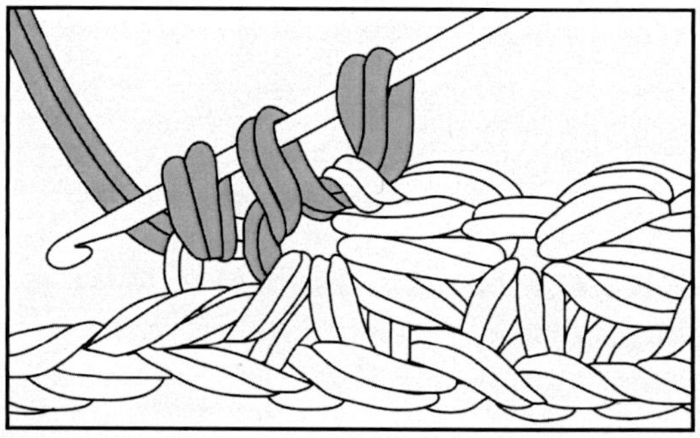

REVERSE SINGLE CROCHET

Working from **left** to **right**, insert hook in stitch to right of hook ***(Fig. 26a)***, YO and draw through, under and to left of loop on hook (2 loops on hook) ***(Fig. 26b)***, YO and draw through both loops on hook ***(Fig. 26c)*** **(reverse sc made, *Fig. 26d*)**.

Fig. 26a

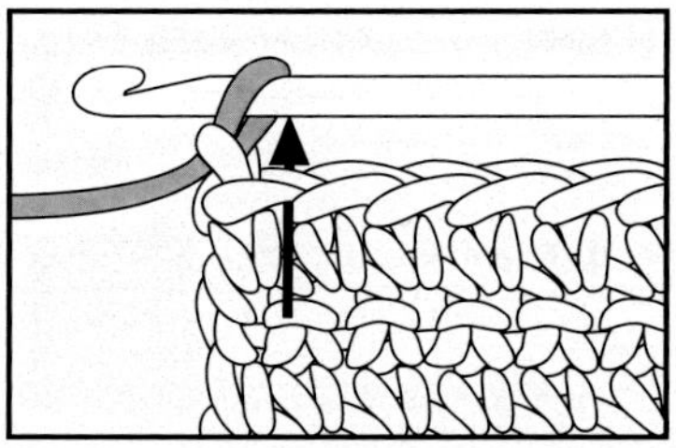

Fig. 26b

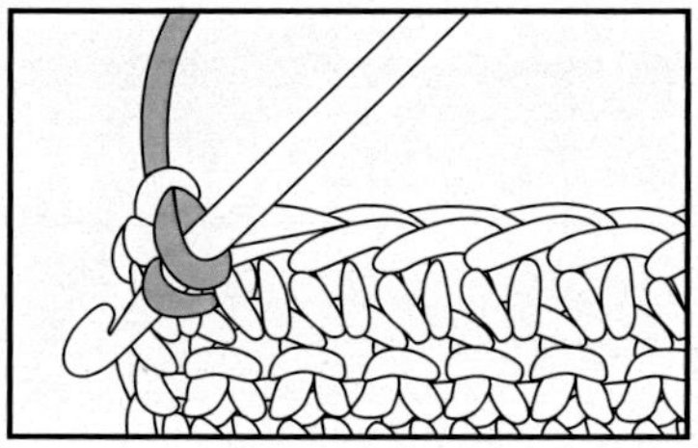

Fig. 26c

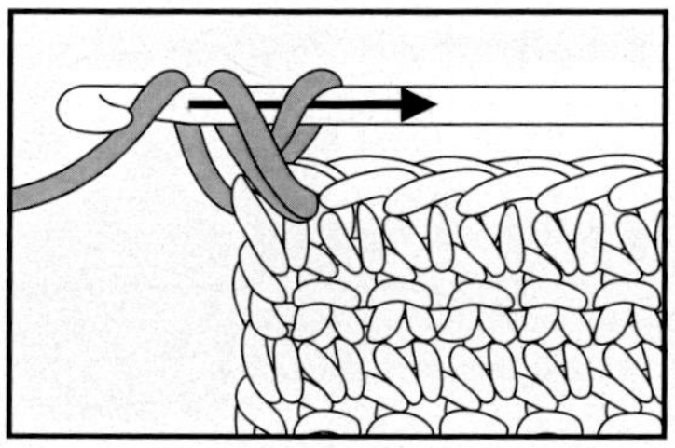

Fig. 26d

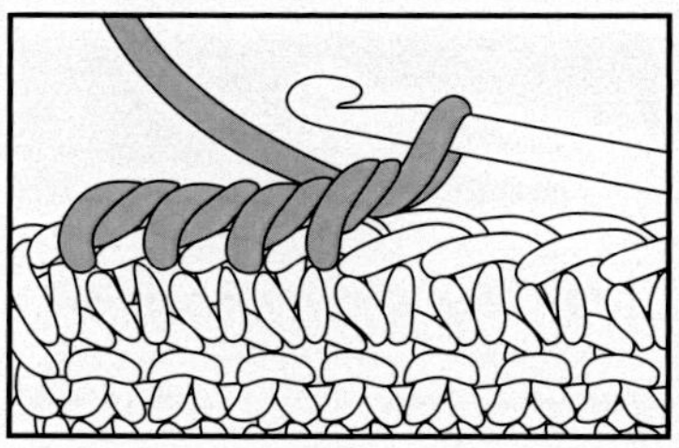

REVERSE HALF DOUBLE CROCHET

Working from **left** to **right**, YO, insert hook in stitch indicated to right of hook ***(Fig. 27a)***, YO and draw through, under and to left of loops on hook (3 loops on hook) ***(Fig. 27b)***, YO and draw through all 3 loops on hook ***(Fig. 27c)*** **(reverse hdc made, *Fig. 27d*)**.

Fig. 27a

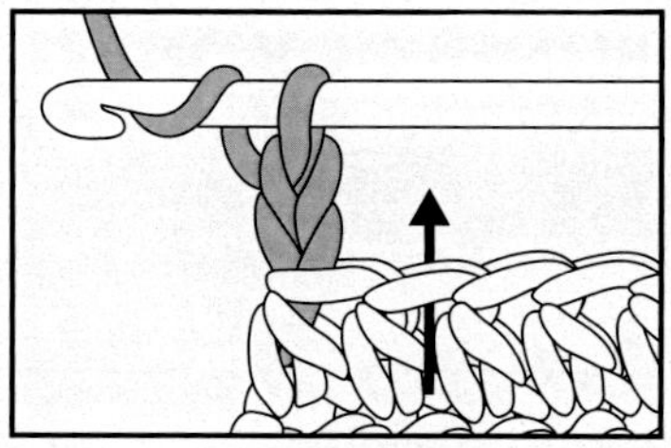

Fig. 27b

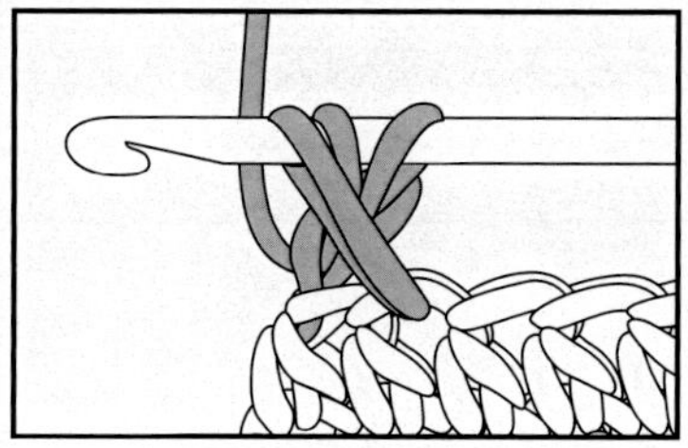

Fig. 27c

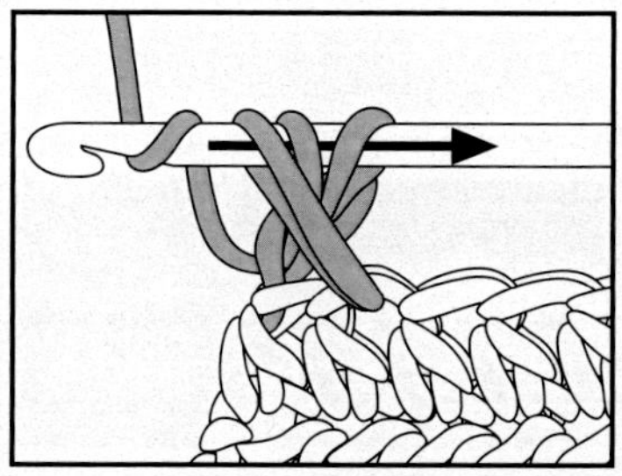

Fig. 26d

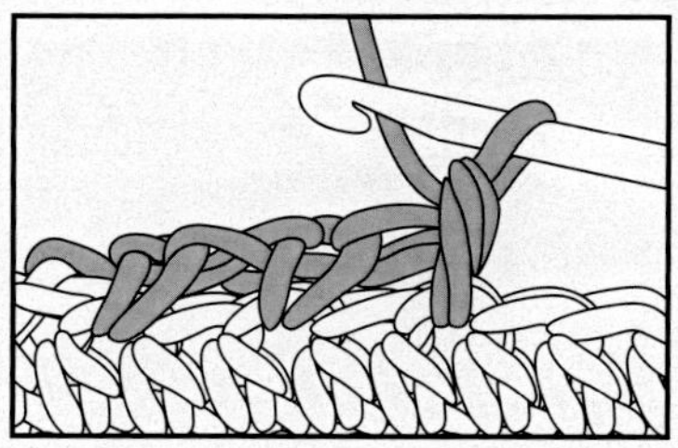

STITCHING TIPS

JOINING WITH SC

When instructed to join with sc, begin with a slip knot on hook. Insert hook in stitch or space indicated, YO and pull up a loop, YO and draw through both loops on hook.

BACK OR FRONT LOOP ONLY

Work only in loop(s) indicated by arrow *(Fig. 28)*.

Fig. 28

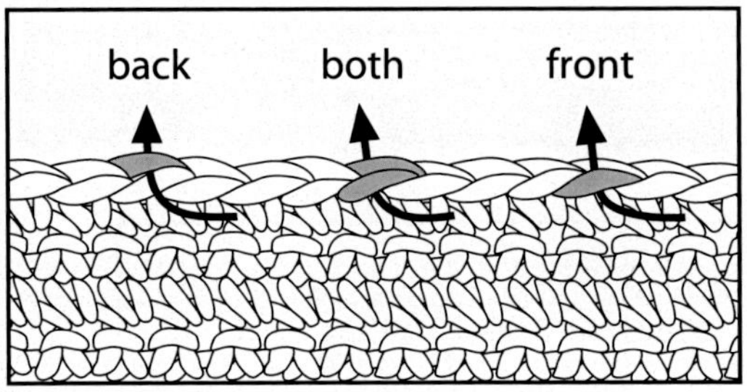

FREE LOOPS

After working in Back or Front Loops Only on a row and round, there will be a ridge of unused loops. These are called the free loops. Later, when instructed to work in the free loops of same row or round, work in these loops *(Fig. 29a)*.

When instructed to work in free loops of a beginning chain, work in loop indicated by arrow *(Fig. 29b)*.

Fig. 29a

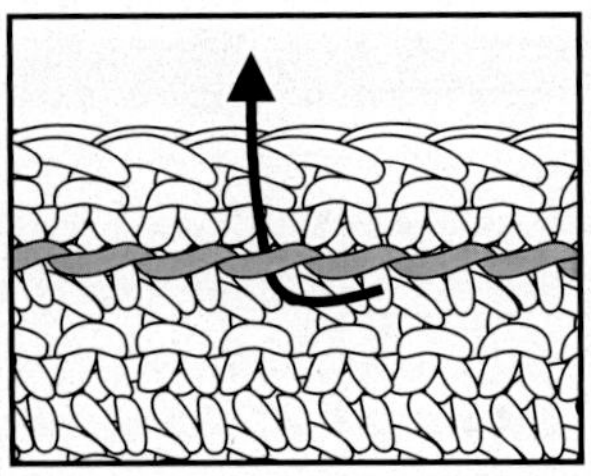

Fig. 29b

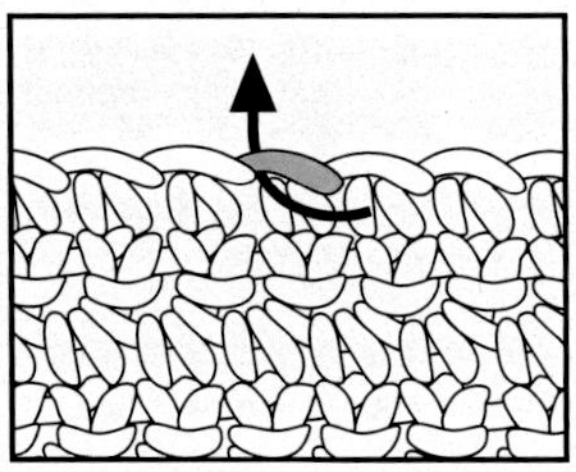

CHANGING COLORS

Work the last stitch to within one step of completion, hook new yarn *(Fig. 30a)* and draw through all loops on hook. Cut old yarn and work over both ends.

When working in rounds, drop old yarn and join with slip stitch to first stitch using new yarn *(Fig. 30b)*.

Fig. 30a

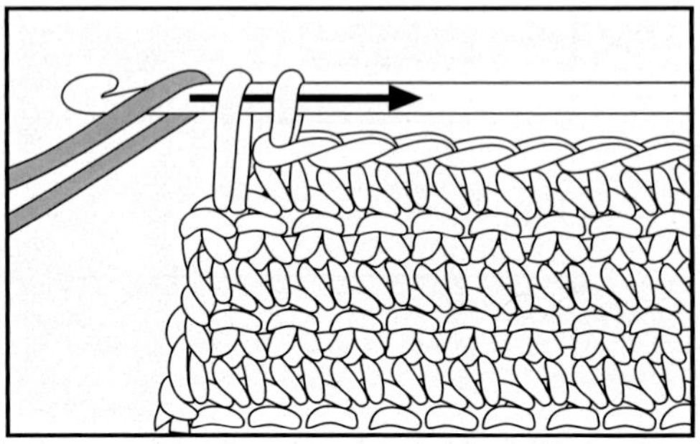

Fig. 30b

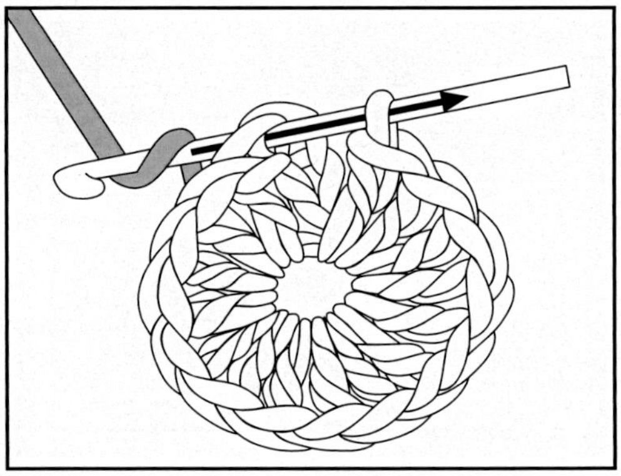

FINISHING

WEAVING

With **wrong** sides together, sew through both pieces once to secure the beginning of the seam, Leaving an ample yarn end to weave in later. Insert the needle from **right** to **left** through one strand on each piece ***(Fig. 31)***. Bring the needle around and insert it from **right** to **left** through the next strand on both pieces.

Repeat along the edge, being careful to match stitches and rows.

Fig. 31

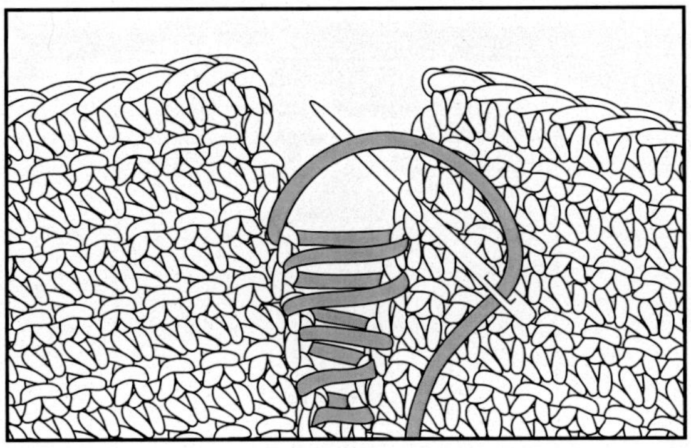

WHIP STITCH

With **wrong** sides together and beginning in corner stitch, sew through both pieces once to secure the beginning of the seam, leaving an ample yarn end to weave in later. Insert the needle from **right** to **left** through **inside** Loops of each piece ***(Fig. 32a)*** or through both Loops ***(Fig. 32b)***. Bring the needle around and insert it from **right** to **left** through the next loops of **both** pieces. Repeat along the edge, keeping the sewing yarn fairly loose and being careful to match stitches.

Fig. 32a

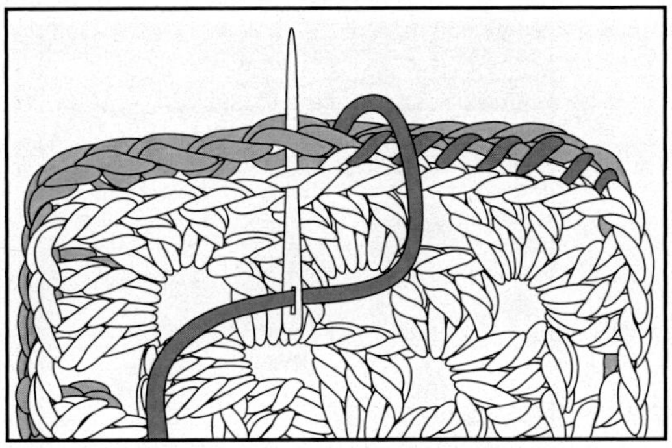

Fig. 32b

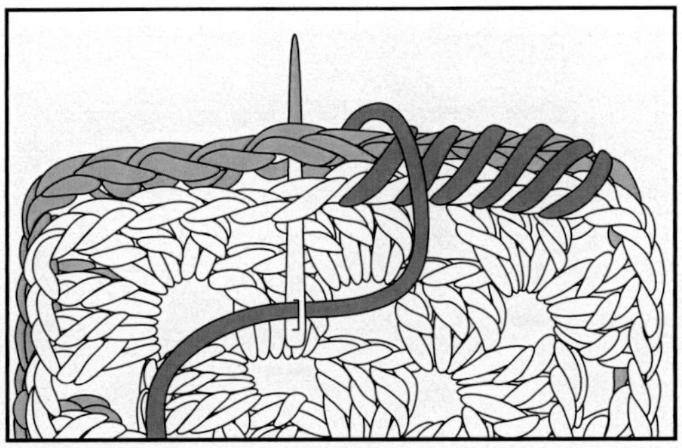

FRINGE

Cut a piece of cardboard 3" wide and half as long as specified in instructions. Wind the yarn **loosely** and **evenly** around the length of cardboard until the card is filled, then cut across one end; repeat as needed.

Hold the number of strands specified for one knot together and fold in half.

With **wrong** side facing and using a crochet hook, draw the folded end up through a stitch or row and pull the loose ends through the folded end ***(Figs. 33a & b)***; draw the knot up **tightly** ***(Figs. 33c & d)***. Repeat, spacing as desired.

Lay flat on a hard surface and trim the ends.

Fig. 33a

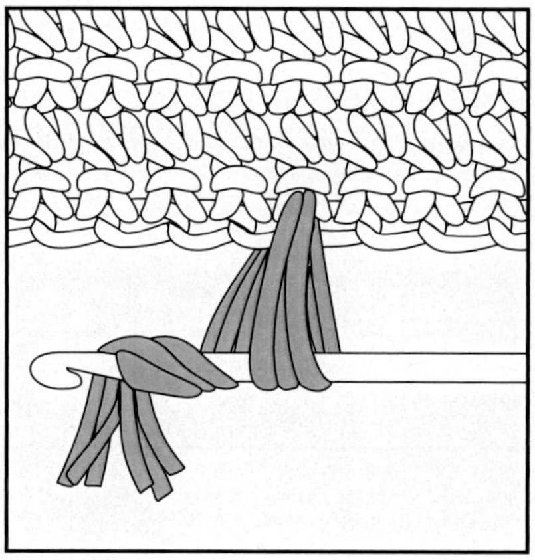

Fig. 33b

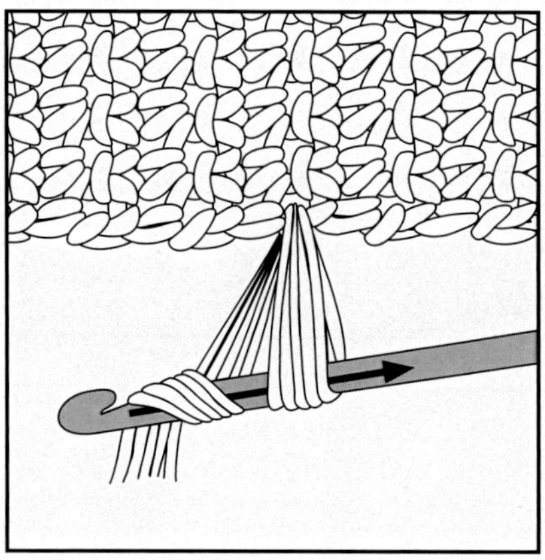

Fig. 33c

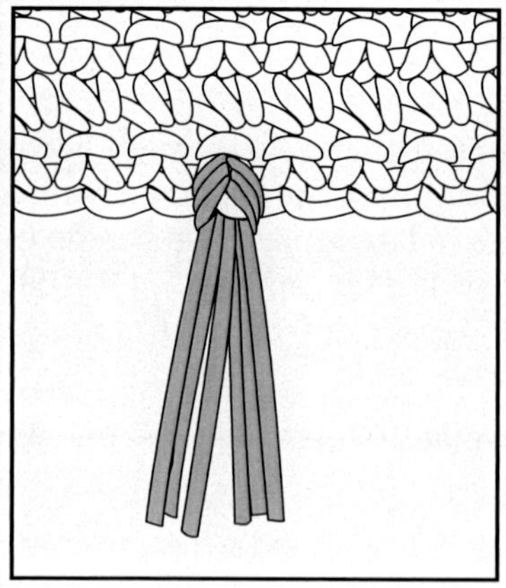

Fig. 33d

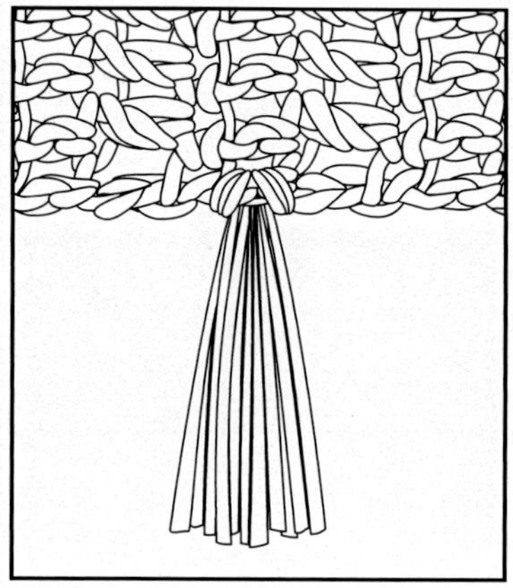

CREDITS

We extend a warm thank you to the generous people who allowed us to photograph some of our afghans at their homes: Bill and Nancy Appleton, Carl and Monte Brunck, Frank and Carol Clawson, Dr. Dan and Sandra Cook, Joan Gould, Shirley Held, Dick and Jan Henry, Dr. Tony Johnson, Nancy Gunn Porter, and Dr. Dudley and Cathy Rodgers, and Dot Woodruff.

Sincere thanks go to Arkansas Landscape and Garden Center of Little Rock, Arkansas, for allowing us to photograph the ***True Blue Ripples*** afghan from the ***Double Play*** section on their property and for allowing us to use their wagon. We would also like to thank Ethan Allen Home Interiors of Little Rock, Arkansas, for allowing us to photograph the ***Peachy Elegance, Fringe Benefits, Checkmate Basketweave,*** and ***Contrasting Interest*** afghans from the ***Distinctively Double*** section at their place of business.

To Magna IV Color Imaging of Little Rock, Arkansas, we say thank you for the superb color reproduction and excellent pre-press preparation.

We want to especially thank photographers Ken West, Larry Pennington, Mark Mathews, and Karen Shirey of Peerless Photography, Little Rock, Arkansas, and Jerry R. Davis of Jerry Davis Photography, Little Rock, Arkansas, for their time, patience, and excellent work.

We would like to extend a special word of thanks to the talented designers who created the lovely projects in this book:

Mary lamb Becker: *Vintage Violets*, page 10; *Old-fashioned Charm*, page 12; and *Bold Heritage*, page 66
Carla Bentley: *Rainbow Stripes*, page 72; *Rainbow Granny*, page 78; and *Blended Rainbow*, page 84
Judy Bolin: N*ine-Patch Granny*, page 30, and *Polka Dot Patch*, page 80
Anne Halliday: *Rugged Wrap*, page 18; *Granny's Delight*, page 24; *Fireside Throw*, page 28; *Wavy Stripes*, page 32; and *Contrasting Interest*, page 64
Carol Janson: *Distinctive Diamonds*, page 62
Shala Johnson: *Rustic Raised Chevron*, page 20; *Checkmate Basketweave*, page 50; and *Captivating Shells*, page 88
Tel'l'y Kimbrough: *Simplicity*, page 106
Linda Luder: *Serene Ripples*, page 60, and *Carefree Filet*, page 70
Kay Fisher Meadors: *Mimosa Blossoms*, page 98
Carole Prior: *Golden Waves*, page 34; *Cascade of Roses*, page 40; *Peachy Elegance*, page 42; *Fringe Benefits*, page 44; *Lacy Trellis*, page 48; *Luxurious Wrap*, page 52; *Discriminating Taste*, page 56; *Nautilus*, page 74; *Sea Peach*, page 82; *Ocean Breeze*, page 100; *Fanciful Fans*, page 102; *Soft Scallops*, page 104; *Stars for Baby*, page 108; and *Spring Awakening*, page 114
Mary Jane Protus: *A Study in Comfort*, page 22, and *Delicate Shells*, page 110
Cheryl Riley: *Baby-Soft Rainbow*, page 96
Mary Anne Sipes: S*outhwestern Stripes*, page 86
Carole Rutter Tippett: *Zigzag Filet*, page 6; *Classic Cables*, page 8; *Lacy Pineapples*, page 26; *Crisscross Cable*, page 46; *Handsome Aran*, page 58; *True Blue Ripple*, page 76; and *Victorian Lace*, page 112
Joyce Winfield Vanderslice: *Double Stair Step*, page 14, and *Hearthside Diamonds*, page 16
Beth Ann Webber: *Charming Wrap*, page 94

We extend a sincere *thank you* to the people who assisted in making and testing many of the projects in this book: Rozlyn Anderson, Belinda Baxter, JoAnn Bowling, Lee Ellis, Linda Galloway, Linda Graves, Naomi Greening, Raymelle Greening, Jean Hall, Kathleen Hardy, Chrys Harvey, Lisa Hightower, Connie Hilton, Ruth Landon, Carolyn Lee, Ruby I.ee, Margie Norris, Dale Potter, Carla Rains, Faith Stewart, Karan Stewart, Clare Stringer, Bill Tanner, Margaret Taverner, Carol Thompson, Debbie Thompson, and Sherry Williams.

Show us what you're working on!

Share your project photos with us on social media.
Tag us @leisureartsinc or use #leisurearts